Dare to Matter

CHOOSING AN UNSTUCK AND UNAPOLOGETIC
LIFE OF SIGNIFICANCE

Pete Smith

Dare to Matter
Copyright © 2016 Pete Smith
All rights reserved

The information presented herein represents the views of the author as of
the date of publication. This book is presented for informational purposes
only. Due to the rate at which conditions change, the author reserves the
right to alter and update his opinions at any time. While every attempt
has been made to verify the information in this book, the author does
not assume any responsibility for errors, inaccuracies, or omissions.

ISBN: 978-0-9984527-0-8 (paperback)
ISBN: 978-0-9984527-1-5 (ebook)

Editing by Carrie Snider and Thomas Hauck
Interior Formatting and Design by Dale Pease at Walking Stick Books
Book Cover Design by Christina Michaelidis with CGM DESIGNS

For Whitney, Finnegan, and Declan

With a single smile,

you make the world seem right again.

CONTENTS

INTRODUCTION

If your life were to end today, would you know with certainty that you mattered?

That you touched other lives?

That you made a difference in the world?

I suppose if you've dedicated your life to feeding the hungry in a developing nation, you might be inclined to answer "yes" to that question.

For the rest of us mere mortals, however, that question can eat away at the very core of who we are. After all, we're just nice, normal people trying to get by—right?

In a world where people are overworked, overwhelmed, and overcommitted, do we even have time to consider such a preposterous question? Does it even matter if we matter?

Deep, right? I know. I feel like I should be reaching for my double Scotch whisky as I write this. Admittedly, I never considered these questions myself—that is, until I almost lost it all. As you'll read inside, my near-death experience turned out to be a pivotal moment in my life.

I was just thirty-five years old at the time. I assumed I had a lot of living left to do.

Over time, I've examined the lives of those with whom I've spent thousands of hours coaching, training, and befriending along the way. I've had the pleasure of speaking to thousands of people from different countries, industries, and companies, and each person I meet possesses a story unique unto themselves.

I've found consistencies and patterns in the way people think, how they act, and the results they produce. While these patterns have helped them achieve the goals they've desired in some aspects of their lives, they're also the reasons why they've fallen short of their desired goals in other aspects of their lives.

The result of this curiosity and observation has led to the creation of the framework, concepts, and practical takeaways presented in this book. This book provides you the opportunity to examine who you are and what you're doing with your life through a lens of significance.

Significance.

It's what you desire, isn't it? If you were just looking for quick tips and short cuts on how to be merely successful, you'd be looking for another book by now; at least, that's what I'd encourage you to do.

It's not that this book won't assist your efforts to become successful. It certainly can. There's more to life than that, however. By following the framework, you'll experience the ultimate desire that doesn't automatically come with one's success: fulfillment.

You and I both know plenty of successful people who aren't happy. The solution to that spiritual and emotional void is revealed in the following pages.

When I decided to write this book, I made an internal promise to leave out what is so often associated with this type of topic: fluff.

There's so much feel-good nonsense being thrown around today. People want to talk about dreams, happiness, and—I don't know—kitten videos, instead of focusing on the things that really matter.

In an effort to feel better, people spend countless hours on Facebook clicking the "like" button for every inspiring quote their friends post. They might even try to fool the world into thinking they are truly as happy as their daily status update says they are.

But are they truly happy? Do they live lives of significance and fulfillment?

Perhaps that's too judgmental on my part. Maybe it's just best to say that this book is a full-contact, no-nonsense guide to get you focused on making a significant difference in this world.

This book is not for the faint of heart. It's for those who are ready to move beyond *thinking* and into *doing*. You may find it to be challenging, enlightening, and even confrontational at times. I encourage you to stick with me until the end. Ultimately, it's up to you to make an important decision: you're either going to go all-in and pursue significance, or you're not.

This book is about action, not knowledge. You'll be best served if you don't simply *read* the book from cover to cover but, rather, *work through* the book cover to cover.

To help with this, I've created a free PDF workbook for you. Go to **www.daretomatterbook.com**, download the workbook, and start putting into action the things you've been dreaming about for too long.

Now is your time.

As you'll read in the upcoming pages, the most profound moment of my life occurred the instant I thought I had sixty seconds left to live.

This book is influenced as much by those sixty seconds as the years that have followed.

What could have been an awful situation has become one of those defining moments that change a life in an instant. It seems right, then, to begin there.

See you on the inside.

1

THE FRAMEWORK

What is a framework?

There are formulas and there are frameworks. $E=MC^2$ is a formula. H_2O is the formula for water, and water will always consist of two parts hydrogen and one part oxygen.

Mathematics is full of formulas. Chemistry is full of formulas. These have been tested, retested, and proven; and the consequences are evident when the formulas are not followed.

But a framework is different. In this book I'm presenting to you a framework for living a life of significance, not a formula.

Frameworks can provide the same desired result that a formula can, but they don't necessarily provide absolute step-by-step directions on how to achieve that result. A discussion on how to raise great kids, for example, could take place within the context of a framework. If you're a parent, you know that your kids didn't come with an owner's manual. There isn't one way to raise good kids.

Teaching people how to become effective managers is done within the context of a framework, laced with stories of best practices and managerial disasters. Even then, there's no one way to manage effectively.

Frameworks can provide boundaries, implied or physical, with clear benefits as well as consequences for traveling outside of those boundaries. If I inform my kids that they can play inside the house, the framework is the house.

Notice, however, that it does not dictate what games they play within the house. They have the freedom to decide that for themselves. If they leave the house, however, there will be consequences. Such is the case for this framework regarding living a life of significance.

Is this the only way to live? I won't even pretend to pass that off as a fact. Even the Bible, though a guide that boldly states the benefits and consequences of heeding or not heeding the advice given, is not a step-by-step formula. And trust me, I'm no apostle responsible for writing anything in the Bible.

What I am sharing here is the framework for living a life of significance.

This is a framework to help you stay focused on the things that matter most, which happen to be the only things that matter anyway.

As the framework indicates, the beauty of living a significant life exists in its simplicity. We often find ways to make the simple confusing. We become mesmerized with bigger words, deeper thoughts, and intellectual theories that make us say, "I see," even when, if we're being honest, we don't have a clue about what any of it means. The simplicity of the framework in this book may surprise you, but that is by design. You can't follow a framework unless you understand and embrace it.

But here's the kicker. The concepts and topics within this framework are simple to understand but not easy to implement. It's easy to acknowledge, for example, that we always have a choice, except when it's more convenient to say, "I didn't have a choice." We dream about taking risks and admire those who do. Yet we shy away from believing that we could ever do something similar, so we choose complacency and conformity.

What makes this framework so attractive is also what can make it so intimidating, which is the ability to operate freely within it. There's something immensely freeing yet incredibly terrifying about possessing such vast free will, isn't there?

Within this framework, you'll discover the answers that will undoubtedly help you both personally and professionally. You can't focus on just one and not the other; a huge aspect of the significant life is to stop pretending that somehow this separation of our personal and professional lives is not only possible, but desirable. This, of course, is not true, and continuing our attempts to keep the two distinctly separate often leads to discouragement and frustration.

The significant life is one lived with the recognition that you are one person involved in multiple facets of your life, none of which require you to be a different person for every occasion. Whether a solid, liquid, or gas, water is still two parts hydrogen and one part oxygen.

Instead of thinking of yourself as different parts of a whole, imagine being who you choose to be in *every aspect* of your life. For some, that idea is inconceivable. For those with a significance lens, it's the only way to live.

Finally, you'll recognize that this framework is not subject to your age, your socioeconomic status, your race, your religion, or any other aspect that makes you think this doesn't apply to you. I assure you, it does, simply because it addresses those aspects of life that connect us at the human being level. If you are a human, it applies to you.

2

911 - WHAT'S YOUR EMERGENCY?

"It is worth dying to find out what life is."

~ T.S. Eliot

It was 6:45 a.m. I was about to walk out of my house and drive to work when I decided to quickly check emails that had come in the night before. Standing at my dining room table, I scanned and responded to the most time-sensitive requests before closing my laptop.

I suddenly felt my legs become strangely weak. I assumed it was because I was tired, having played softball late the night before and getting an early start to my morning.

My weak legs became wobbly, then useless. I fell backwards. I was able to twist my body enough to grab the chair behind me for support, temporarily. But my body weight was too much for one arm to support and I lost my balance.

"Whitney!" I yelled as I went crashing to the ground, landing in a sitting position.

I sat in a daze, the world swirling around me. I'd been exhausted before. I'd been dizzy. I'd even been fall-over drunk, but I never felt quite like that. Something was different. People my age didn't just fall for no reason.

My mind was racing to figure out an answer to what was happening to me. I knew I wasn't having a heart attack. Other than a faster heart rate due to my panicking, I didn't feel the heavy weight on my chest, as those who have experienced heart attacks describe.

Was this a seizure? I'm not sure why I thought that. I've never had a seizure in my life. I don't think I could recognize a seizure if I had one.

When you're suddenly and inexplicably incapacitated, your brain tries to make sense of it. But such a life-altering event rarely makes sense, and so you're just left with confusion.

In the midst of frantically searching for but never quite finding an answer to what was happening, my mind quickly focused on something terrifying: A noise.

I heard my body shutting down.

Internally I could hear it, like the sound of an engine winding down. Think about turning off a lawnmower, about the sound the motor makes while winding down. The gears tiring and going slower and slower until they were to reach a stop. Internally, that's what it sounded like to me. My body was winding down. I didn't just sense that it was shutting down; I heard it shutting down.

A fall was one thing, but this was another thing entirely.

No, no, no, no, no! Stop. This isn't happening. This can't be happening.

I struggled to remain sitting upright, as it seemed my body preferred that I let myself lay down. I was able to use my left arm to keep from tipping over in that direction. In my head, I was adding up the damage. The fact that my body wanted to lay down and curl up wasn't a good sign.

I had always been taught to fight, to go after what I wanted. But as I learned in this moment, I was not in control.

I felt trapped, in a claustrophobic way. Yet there was no physical containment. I wanted to break free but I didn't know exactly what was restraining me. I was fighting an enemy that I couldn't see, grab, or talk to. But I knew for certain that the enemy was real, and it was winning.

There was nothing I could do to stop the decline. I could feel my internal engine wanted to stop completely, and I couldn't get the engine started again. In that moment, I had a very real, concise thought:

I'm dying.

I wanted to burst into tears. No, more than that. I wanted to sob; sob like someone who, probably for the first time in his life, realized that he couldn't stop time. There were no more "do-overs" or "time outs." Sob like someone who finally and fully understands what it feels like to be utterly hopeless and helpless.

Amidst the panic and the chaos of random thoughts racing inside my head, I suddenly had a moment of absolute calm and clarity.

I thought about Whitney.

I thought about how she was going to come down the stairs, turn the corner, and see me dead on my dining room floor. I wondered how she would handle that.

Whitney had been married once, before we met. We were introduced by a mutual friend while she was separated. We dated for a couple of years, got engaged, and were scheduled to get married just five months from the day this was happening.

I wondered how she was going to feel with a marriage ending in divorce and an engagement ending in death. I felt so sad for her and so guilty for being the cause of her new pain.

Would she think that her relationships are doomed, and therefore never try again? She was too good of a person to have this happen to her, I thought. She didn't deserve this.

I thought about my parents, my brothers, and sisters. My family.

I wondered how my parents would handle the news that I died that morning. I thought about which brother or sister would be the one to tell them, and I wondered about the impact this would have on that person moving forward.

All of those thoughts raced through my head at tremendous speed, but then my mind stopped for a second. In the moment you're dying, your brain has to divert a lot of attention to fixing itself. As a result, your mind lets go of everything that doesn't matter.

I reached a moment of supreme clarity. And that's when I asked myself a simple, yet powerful question:

Did I live?

Immediately upon asking myself that question, it was followed by a series of thoughts and questions related to that question.

Did people I love know I loved them?

Did I do everything I wanted to do in this life?

Did I hold back?

Did I change anyone's life?

Am I going to heaven?

I'm not ready for this.

Please, not now. Not yet.

What I find so interesting about those questions and random thoughts was that at no time did I ever once consider whether or not I was successful.

Never once.

I don't even recall thinking about whether I was "happy."

In a way, I suppose both of those things seemed too superficial at the time, even though society continues to send this message that our two greatest endeavors in life are the achievement of both success and happiness. How minimizing!

Experts have long discussed whether happiness leads to success or success leads to happiness. They have manifested theories and best practices about how to achieve both. People have placed an enormous amount of their energy, time, attention, and money to achieve both of these.

I'm convinced that we're focused on the wrong outcomes. During those critical moments, I never once thought about success.

Instead, I thought about whether I was *significant.*

At the precise moment when I thought my life was ending, one of the things that mattered to me most was whether or not I mattered at all.

Did I matter?

"Pete?" Whitney called out from the top of the stairs. "Did you call me?"

I tried to respond to her but couldn't. I had lost the ability to speak.

"Pete?" she called again.

Come downstairs, I thought. *Just come downstairs.*

She did.

As Whitney turned the corner, our eyes met. I'm sure my eyes portrayed fear and sorrow and clarity all at the same time. I attempted to tell her to call 911, as if the fact that I couldn't say anything wasn't already a clear indicator that she probably should. No words formed with my mouth, but she got the message.

She quickly called 911. As she knelt in front of me, I heard only her side of the conversation with the dispatcher.

"Hi. I need your help. My fiancé is on the ground. He can't speak." She was incredibly calm, or at least she appeared to be.

She gave them my address and answered a few questions.

There was a pause, and then she spoke again. "A stroke? I'm not sure. How...."

My mind trailed off, not paying attention to what was said next.

I'm having a stroke? I thought. *That can't be. Old people have strokes. Smokers have strokes. No one in my family has strokes. That can't be right.*

"I'm not sure. Let me check," I heard Whitney say, as I focused on her again. I looked down at her hand. She was touching my right arm, which was folded in my lap. I didn't feel a thing.

It's an eerie feeling to see someone touching you and having absolutely no connection to that body part whatsoever. It's as if someone else's arm was resting on my lap.

Besides falling and my internal engine slowing to a near stop, now I couldn't talk and I couldn't feel my right arm.

Through my dining room window, I could hear sirens outside. Luckily, an ambulance was nearby and speeding towards my house.

Knowing help was on its way, I felt a sense of comfort. I finally allowed my body to lay down on the hard dining room floor. The sound of my internal engine winding down had disappeared, though I can't recall exactly when that sound stopped.

Whitney sat by my side.

"I love you," she told me.

The best I could do was extend a half-hearted smile. I pointed to a piece of paper and pen that was situated nearby. Whitney somehow understood what I was asking for and gave it to me. I tried to write with my left hand.

That didn't work well. I'm a hardcore righty. Even when I'm not officially having a stroke, if you tried reading my handwriting when using my left hand, you'd swear I was having a stroke.

I dropped the pen in disgust. Panic gave way to anger. I couldn't speak. I couldn't move my dominant side, and I couldn't even write on a piece of paper. I figured I'd need a chalkboard around my neck for the rest of my life like Anthony Hopkins had after his stroke in the movie *Legends of the Fall*.

The paramedics arrived and, after a series of tests, questions, and decisions, they lifted my inert body onto a stretcher and loaded me into the ambulance. I was on my way to the hospital.

While in route, I started to move my fingers. I also began to whisper. Not long after I arrived at the hospital, most of my speech returned and I could move my arm again completely. I almost felt apologetic that they were rushing me into the hospital so quickly. It seemed like a false alarm.

After multiple exams and tests taken between two different hospitals that day, the scans revealed a clot in the middle cerebral artery that had caused the speech, sensory, and movement issues. But the scans also revealed that the brain was redirecting blood flow around the clot, paving the way for the return of my speech and bodily movement. Fascinating!

On my third day in the hospital, a final test revealed a small hole in my heart, one that apparently I've had since birth. This hole, found in the wall between the heart's two upper chambers, is called a *patent foramen ovale*, or PFO. Though the doctors could not state with certainty that this hole was the reason for the stroke, it seemed to be a reasonable possibility.

Therefore, mostly as a precautionary measure, one month later I had my PFO closed.

I've felt great ever since. I consider it a miracle.

Some people who have survived similar events report that the grass becomes greener and the air becomes fresher to them. For a brief period of time after my stroke, I would concur with those sentiments.

But I don't mean to pretend that every day is a "Snow White" day, where I sing joyously along a nature trail while wild animals flock to me because of my pure goodness.

I still experience frustrations, and anger, and sadness. I experience joy, and laughter, and happiness. I am still human. But some things are different.

My relationship with time has shifted. Perhaps to a fault, I am more inclined to live in the present than being content to wait five or ten years to pursue something important to me.

My relationship with control has definitely changed. I realize now that we actually control very little in our lives, though we try to convince ourselves otherwise.

Money and success have taken their rightful place in my life. I do not pretend that neither of them is important. Quite the contrary. They matter to me quite a bit. But it's not the just the achievement of both that's important. It's why I wish to pursue those things, how I go about achieving them, and what I do once I have them, which are the ultimate revelations of character. It's what prompts me to consistently look in the mirror daily, to challenge the person looking back to become better for the betterment of others.

Reflecting on the stroke, I'm so appreciative of that entire experience. Yes, it was terrifying, but it was so much more than that. I am humbled. I am grateful. I am enlightened. I am energized.

The framework described in the previous chapter has resulted from examining my thoughts in the moment when I was convinced my life was ending. It is more than that, however. It is a call to action. It is a challenge, a plea, and a request of you to evaluate, assess, and transform your life in accordance with the things that matter most.

No longer is it acceptable to procrastinate, to attempt to convince ourselves that someday our lives will be the way we want them to be.

No longer can we stand idly as life speeds past us in the blink of an eye. We must refuse to acquiesce to the tempting allure of conformity and complacency.

We must recognize that though we have one chance at this life, we have multiple opportunities to reinvent who we are and what we do in this life.

By choosing for ourselves what we will make our lives, we get to experience that which is written on the heart of every man: the calling, the drive, the yearning to contribute and make a significant difference.

It is clear to me that what connects us all as human beings, deep within our core, is a great desire to know with certainty that who we are and what we do matters.

We want to matter and we want to live a life that matters.

Anyone who says otherwise has either not been faced with their own mortality or they're afraid of admitting that they have fallen short of who they were created to be.

The good news is, you don't have to be dying to get some clarity. Enlightenment and understanding come to us through a variety of sources. But clarity alone won't bring about a significant life. It still requires that you decide what is meaningful in your life and pursue it with every ounce of energy you can muster.

Through recognition of death, I was taught about life. These insights I share with you. The question that remains is what you choose to do with it.

3

ALWAYS A CHOICE

"In the long run, we shape our lives, and we shape ourselves. The process never ends until we die. And the choices we make are ultimately our own responsibility."

~ Eleanor Roosevelt

It starts with you.

You always have a choice, and your choices are the only thing you actually control. Nothing more. Nothing less.

Have you heard of Liz Murray? She's the author of *Breaking Night*. You might be more familiar with her story of how she went from homeless to Harvard.

Liz was born in New York to drug addicted parents. Her mom died of AIDS, her dad moved into a homeless shelter, and her sister moved in with her abusive grandfather. A high school dropout herself, at the age of sixteen Liz was homeless on the streets of New York.

At the age of seventeen, Liz chose to complete her high school education. She enrolled at the Humanities Preparatory School, a new progressive public school in downtown Manhattan.

While still enrolled in high school, Murray's story attracted the attention of the New York Times Scholarship Program. This fund focuses on students who have overcome significant hardships in their lives and gives them the opportunity to attend top-tier universities, including the Ivy League schools. Murray was accepted into Harvard, and in the fall of 2000 started her first semester.

Reflecting on her road to Harvard, here's what Liz said about her journey in a YouTube video:[1]

> When I describe how I grew up to people, there's almost like two ways to look at it. I grew up like most people did, with a family surrounding me in a home filled with love. It just so happened that mom and dad were addicted to cocaine and heroin. My mom was an alcoholic, and we had this drug addiction like a wrecking ball, tearing through our family.
>
> When I lost everything, I was invigorated in this way where I realized my life was actually just a blank slate, and in that space which came to me in a very painful way, this freedom opened up to really just declare, well, what do I want my life to be about? ... I realized that life could be so much more than ordinary.

What I've learned is that actually no one knows what's possible until they do it.... You don't know. No one knows, and that's what's kind of cool about life. That's what's so beautiful is that every single day is another chance.

Most of us will never experience anything close to what Liz experienced. I have a difficult time even comprehending the enormity and seriousness of her situation. I hope to never be tested similarly. But her outcome is encouraging.

Because of the choices she made in her past, she is presently a best-selling author and well-known speaker. A made-for-TV film about Murray's life, *Homeless to Harvard: The Liz Murray Story*, was released in 2003. Her story is indicative of our power to choose. Liz chose to make something more of her life, even when her living situation could have provided plenty of convincing reasons to give up.

Like Liz, things have happened in your life that you didn't choose. But also like Liz, you are where you are because of the choices you have made. The good in your life, the bad in your life—all of it is directly connected to your previous choices. Even in those situations when you chose not to choose, that was still a choice.

You may not be a best-selling author or the focus of a documentary film, but you may feel inclined to give yourself a pat on the back if you're pretty satisfied with what you've been able to accomplish so far. Or you may be entertaining the idea of launching this book across the room if things haven't exactly worked out as you hoped. Perhaps there's even some guilt about the choices you have made and the results you have produced.

As you reflect on your life, I imagine you can identify some choices that had a direct, and largely influential, impact in the direction of your life. For example, if you're married, one person chose to propose and the other chose to accept. That's a big choice. But before the engagement happened, think of all the choices that you made, seemingly insignificant choices, which led to that moment.

Think about how you met that person. Did you meet at a bar, or party, or grocery store? You made a choice to go to that exact spot on that exact day at that exact moment.

It could have been a choice that didn't require much forethought. Perhaps you've been to that place many times before. Maybe it was your first time. I doubt, however, you made the decision with the understanding that this was the moment you were going to meet someone with whom you would choose to spend the rest of your life. Having known that, some people might have chosen otherwise!

My point is that we make many choices every day, all with varying degrees of impact on our lives. We can identify some choices that carry a substantial impact, while others may seem inconsequential. Regardless, all choices led you to this very moment.

Like the past, your present and future life will be influenced by the choices you make today. If you want to experience more personal freedom in your life, it begins with the recognition that you always have a choice. The more you embrace and live this, the more freedom you experience. There is something magical—euphoric, even—to be able to stand up and say, "I choose," and then act accordingly.

Most people understand this at the conceptual level. We nod our heads in agreement that, yes, we always have the ability to choose and that our choices generate results, positive and negative.

Understanding that is easy. Accepting, admitting, and applying it can be much more difficult, especially when we're in situations when we don't like our options. Always having a choice does not mean you will always like your options.

It's the lack of likable options when our ownership, our responsibility, of making choices becomes difficult to accept. It's easier to say, even believe, that you don't have a choice in certain situations. Of course, as you'd guess by now, this thinking is incorrect.

But what if the options are so heavily weighted that it appears that you really didn't have a choice, that the decision was almost a foregone conclusion? Let's explore this.

Let's imagine Kathy, a single mom of two kids. She works as an entry level employee for a local company. She has expressed her frustration about work to her friends. She is mistreated and micromanaged by her manager. She likes her coworkers—most of them, anyway—but often thinks about what it would be like to work somewhere else. Financially, she earns enough to cover the monthly bills, but she hasn't been able to save much.

After yet another difficult day at work, Kathy decides to explore alternative working opportunities. Unfortunately, she finds very few openings for positions in her area commensurate with her qualifications and experience. The few opportunities that are available are located hours from her home. Thinking about the before-and-after school care service that she would need to cover the additional commuting time, Kathy recognizes that she doesn't have the financial resources to pay for that. She feels depressed, defeated, and frustrated.

In this case, does Kathy really have a choice? It seems that she doesn't have the luxury of quitting her job because she's a great mom who wants to ensure her kids continue to have food and shelter. Staying at her current job seems to be her only option.

Even in this type of scenario, Kathy still has a choice. She has options. She can choose to leave or she can choose to stay. She's choosing to stay. And then every day, she can choose how she will perform at her job.

That may sound harsh and void of any empathetic feeling whatsoever. Not so. Making an exception for one situation, however justified it appears, only makes it easier to view other difficult situations in a similar way and disregard the opportunity of ownership. Assessing any difficult situation from the perspective of the passive victim, the one who continues to have life "done to her," is exactly the opposite of what a significant mindset stands for.

The only thing worse than saying, "I didn't have a choice," is actually believing that it's true.

Now, I'll admit that the options described in my scenario above don't leave Kathy with great choices. Each is less than ideal. Even imagining this scenario as I write it conjures up emotions of empathy, frustration, and a desire to help make it better for her. I also have a few choice words for her fictitious micro-manager.

I hear friends of mine, schoolteachers, describing their work situation as feeling as if they are "stuck" or "trapped." Regarding the requirements for receiving retirement benefits from their respective systems, I often hear them say something like, "The county keeps us here for thirty years," or "That's how the school system traps you."

Hearing that makes me want to crawl out of my skin. They are giving ownership to their feelings on the matter, and not on the actual facts.

The school system has not forced anyone to stay in their jobs. They voluntarily chose to work there. The employee's choice, then, is to either stay working in accordance with the outlined retirement regulations, or don't. It really is that simple. Stay or don't stay. That's the choice.

It's not surprising, and actually quite natural, that our views of our options heavily influence our emotions around whether or not we truly believe we have a choice. However, the level of your responsibility in making decisions is not directly proportional to how much you like your options. Your responsibility is always one hundred percent. You always have a choice, even in those situations where you don't always like your options.

NOT MY FAULT

What about those moments in life that truly aren't your fault? I'm not suggesting you choose to be responsible for those as well, am I?

I am, and here's why: "Responsibility" and "fault" are not one in the same. There are things that happen that may not be your fault, but you can be responsible for something that isn't your fault. "Not my fault" does not automatically grant you "not my responsibility."

If a hurricane were to destroy my house, that act of nature is clearly not my fault. I could go to the extreme and wallow in how irresponsible I was for not building a hurricane resistant house, but this isn't about being a self-loathing, repugnant masochist.

If this were to happen, it is still my responsibility to find shelter for my family. I'm still responsible for their well-being. I still have responsibilities even in those areas that may not have been my fault.

See that "person" sitting next to you at work, the one who has you questioning the existence of God because you're convinced that no God could ever create such an annoying human? You probably didn't hire him. You certainly didn't assign that seat to him. His very existence and presence in the office drives you to think evil thoughts.

His being there may not be your choice or your fault.

He is, however, your responsibility.

You can choose how you interact with him. You can choose how much you allow him to affect you. You can choose how you respond to him. You can still be responsible for the really terrible things in your life, even the ones that came to be outside of your control or desire.

Too many people believe they cannot be successful or significant because of their circumstances.

They say, "I can't go to the gym because I work too much. I can't excel at work because my manager sucks. I can't start my own business because I have two kids. I'm not making enough money because I wasn't given a raise. I can't develop myself because my company doesn't pay for training. I didn't graduate because my teachers never liked me."

These are just lame and cowardly stories people tell themselves to minimize the pain, guilt, and frustration of not being where they want to be, and these people are void of any responsibility or ownership for having chosen to stay exactly where they are.

For some people, there is a tendency to find external reasons that are the cause of their unfortunate, current situation. There's always *something else* or *someone else* who is responsible. The danger with this type of thinking is the assumption that in order for a particular circumstance to improve, the solution must also exist in some external fashion. If someone is constantly looking *externally* at all the reasons why their life sucks, why would they ever begin to look *internally* for a possible solution?

People who consistently look outside themselves for answers often rely on the power of hope, and the hope that at some point someone or something will provide them with a little luck they so desperately need. In their eyes, it's luck that can bring the opportunities and happiness into their life, not their own strength, resolve, and ability.

Relying on such external and unwarranted hope elevates the possibility of experiencing deeper disappointment when the results don't match the desire. If our hope rests in others, so too does our blame of them when they don't come through for us. It's an utter denial of the internal freedom we were given as a birthright, and the absence of such freedom is what true suffering is about.

It's difficult to comprehend and accept that individuals can be the cause of their own limitations, yet that's precisely the most common case. They limit themselves in the way they think, the things they do, the words they use, the people they associate with, and the dreams they suppress. They choose to give away the power to generate a better life to others, without recognizing that that power was never theirs to give away initially.

Empowerment and freedom begin with the recognition that no one is out to get you, but no one is out to rescue you, either. Contrary to those who choose to stay stuck in their current situation, there are plenty of significant people who succeed in life in spite of their circumstances. That begins with the internal choice to make something different in their life.

Hollywood makes a fortune off movies with these types of stories.

Rocky is about a character who was just a boxer with limited intellect. He had a huge heart, great work ethic, and a desire to give it everything he had.

Rudy tells the story of Daniel "Rudy" Ruettiger, a small kid with a deep desire to play football for Notre Dame. His first obstacle was that he couldn't even get into the school. Then, once he worked hard to get accepted, he could only make the practice squad. Finally, he was given a chance to play in a game, even if only for a limited time.

Miracle on Ice was the story of the 1980 USA ice hockey team. Competing against the bigger and stronger Russian team, their defeat seemed inevitable. However, the group of college men came together to defeat the mighty Russians, despite tremendous odds.

You don't need to see a Hollywood blockbuster for these types of stories, even though both *Rudy* and *Miracle on Ice* were inspired by true events. In addition to Liz Murray, there are other examples. Dr. Ben Carson exemplifies someone who elevated himself despite his difficult circumstances. He was raised in poverty and yet became a world-class neurosurgeon.

We love these stories because we appreciate the strength and resolve of the human spirit. We admire and acknowledge the people who overcome such substantial obstacles. We love stories that focus on the hardships individuals face and their willingness to not only address their situation directly, but overcome the odds to achieve victory.

Yet when faced with our own adversity, the temptation can be to withdraw and succumb to our hopeless perception of the circumstance. People too often spend more time making excuses, placing blame, or rationalizing why they can't possibly move ahead because of their current situation than they do proactively doing something about it.

It's time to wake up.

Resilience isn't something you were born with. It's something you develop. We all possess the same ability to make choices that advance our lives in a positive direction. It's time to stop waiting for other people to solve your problems.

The longer you stay stuck in those unfortunate situations that you say aren't your fault, the longer you remain in a mental state of being "done to." This mentality is the battle cry of the victim, and there's nothing significant about being a victim.

EVEN IN HARDSHIP

Perhaps accepting personal responsibility in every situation has been difficult to accept so far. Maybe it's been easy. Regardless, I'm about to take you one step deeper.

I'm going to ask you to consider doing something that at first might seem ludicrous or even senseless, but stick with me.

Think about those situations in your life that have created the most hardship, difficulty, and sleepless nights. The toughest of the tough. The ones that are most likely to get you feeling enraged, hurt, or scared to the point of tears.

As you have this situation vivid in your mind, and with your emotions swirling about, I want you to take a deep breath, close your eyes and verbally say, "I choose this."

Are you dealing with an illness? Choose it.

Going through a divorce? Choose it.

Loss of a loved one? Choose it.

If there's any situation where you've been thinking or saying, "I didn't ask for this," that's exactly the situation I'm encouraging you to choose.

Please understand that this is not an attempt to minimize, discredit, or invalidate any emotions you have around your situation. I do not mean to come across as glib, indifferent, or insincere. Quite the opposite.

There are traumatic events in people's lives that generate a variety of deep, strong emotions. Death. Abuse. Health issues. Divorce. At first, it may seem ridiculous to choose something so devastating in your life, yet that's precisely the only way you'll ever move forward.

I would suspect that there are some people who will think, "Easy for you to say. You haven't experienced_____ (whatever the hardship is)." To an extent, and depending on what you're referring to, you're probably right.

As a parent, I would presume that one of the most difficult situations you would ever encounter is dealing with the loss of a child. The mere thought of that terrifies me. Yet even in those situations, when the timing is right, ultimately, you still have a choice.

I think it's imperative to acknowledge that this isn't about me telling anyone how I think they should grieve in a situation like that. To pretend I can remotely understand what someone else goes through when dealing with that type of loss is both pretentious and hurtful to those who have.

Being aware of this, I reached out to a friend of mine, Paula Stephens, to get her perspective. She continues to live with the loss of her adult son and wrote about it in her book, *Grief to Growth*.

Paula talked about her emotional state after she lost Brandon, who passed away while home on leave from the Army. As she described it to me, it was "way too overwhelming. There was just too much sadness. My whole context of the future was instantly reframed."

About two years after Brandon's death, Paula recognized that she had a choice to make. She told me, "I can choose how I want to keep Brandon's memory alive."

With that, Paula started Crazy Good Grief, a support group for those who have lost a loved one. As she indicates on her website, "I believe we need to live in the sunshine of our loved one's life, not hide in the shadow of their death."

The phenomenon that people can get stronger in the wake of significant tragedy or drama is called post-traumatic growth (PTG), a term coined by Richard Tedeschi, Ph.D., a professor of psychology at the University of North Carolina at Charlotte, and his colleague, Lawrence Calhoun, PhD.

I do not pretend to be an expert in the theory of PTG. The best I can surmise about this phenomenon is that once someone deals with the feelings of loss, anger, resentment, and other emotional pains triggered by the traumatic event, the opportunity for reflection, change, and growth can occur in their lives in substantial ways. That result I can attest to wholeheartedly.

Some people talk about resiliency as being able to bounce back after an event like this. I don't think that's an accurate description. I'm not sure anyone entirely bounces back to where they were before an event like this happens. It's not possible to bounce back to where you were before a traumatic event because you're never the same person after the traumatic event.

Instead, I think resiliency is finding a way to move forward while incorporating all that has happened to you.

Clearly, PTG is not an attempt to make everything better, to make all of the pain go away. I do think, however, it gives hope to those who have struggled, or continue to struggle, with a difficult situation. You can come back stronger. You can repurpose your life. You still have a choice.

A temptation that is paramount to avoid is to compare the severity of your hardship with others. This is both a winning and losing battle. If you believe that no one can ever fully understand the depths of your grief and situation, you are correct. No one can know exactly how you feel.

But to play the "no one has it as bad as I do" game is also a losing battle. There will always be someone out there who, on some surface level, could appear to have suffered more than you. Does a parent who loses two children feel more grief and pain than those who "only" lose one? The mere suggestion of that is ridiculous.

Does a parent who loses a child in infancy suffer less because they haven't built a long relationship with that child? Or do they suffer more because they never had the chance to develop a long relationship with their child?

You see how there is no right or wrong answer, thereby making any comparison both a winning and losing battle. There are no prizes for this competition, nor do I think there would ever be voluntary participants.

What's important is that, regardless of your current circumstance or previous experiences, a life of significance begins with the recognition that you always have a choice. When you are ready for it, there is even a choice in hardship.

The foundation, and recognition, of choice is crucial because it places the only thing you actually control back in your hands. This is a calling and a challenge for everyone to rise from the depths of shallow thinking, conformity, and complacency, and choose a life of meaning.

Choice alone does not necessarily change a life. It must be closely followed by action. But no lasting change in a person's life ever begins without first choosing to do something different with their life.

Yes, with choice come consequences. We cannot embrace the former and deny the latter. For many it's the consequences, whether they're a forethought or a reality, that cause many people to shy away from their responsibilities. This is the plight of the drifter, the whiner, the entitled. He is a lifeless creature, chained to the depths of despair, raging against humanity and everyone in it, all while holding the key to the lock in his hands.

Own your choices. Own the consequences. Own your life.

Live a life where you choose who you want to be. Choose the characteristics that embody every bit of good within you. Choose to address the fears that have internally enslaved you for years. Choose to break free of the chains of righteousness, and martyrdom, and victimhood. Choose to embark on adventures that align with what you deem to be meaningful in your life. Choose to live a significant life, one that ultimately concludes with the impact you have on others.

These are the choices that lead to a life of significance. There are very few spoken words more powerful than the words "I choose" and nothing more powerful than a purpose-driven person.

4

ROOTED IN IDENTITY

And God said to Moses, "I Am who I Am."

~ Exodus 3:13-15 (NLV)

Have you ever considered the source of your actions? If you're like many people, myself included, you may recognize that much of what you do is influenced by how you feel.

When I feel happy, for example, I'm inclined to act in a manner consistent with someone who feels happy. I smile more. My outlook for the day is more positive. I initiate conversation.

I feel, therefore I do.

Then, because I'm acting happy, I can say, "I am happy." My actions are creating my identity.

I feel, therefore I do. I do, therefore I am. It starts with feelings, moves into actions, and ends with identity.

Seems natural. Rational, even. Right? And that's where the problem lies.

Thinking that your behavior is nothing more than the product of your feelings is a reactive, disempowering, and, quite honestly, terrifying thought. Feelings are anything but stable. Have you ever spent time with middle or high school kids, especially the ones worked up over the latest school drama? Listening as they retell the "horrors" of what so-and-so said to so-and-so generates a deep-seated desire to jab myself in the jugular. I look for the director, wondering when he will appear behind the curtain and yell, "... And, cut." What a theatrical scene!

There is nothing consistent, or even predictable to an extent, about feelings. You know this. It's the reason why, on most days, you're a very calm person. But when you get cut off in traffic, you immediately grow fangs and start snarling like a cornered animal.

If we believe that we don't control our feelings, and our feelings are the source of our actions, why would we possibly be expected to think we actually have any control over our behavior? We're like seaweed, swaying every which way the tide flows.

If our identity is shaped by our behavior, which is influenced by something we have little control over, how can we possibly expect to have any control over who we actually are?

A life lived in this manner is simply going through the motions. It's built on the hope that we wake up every morning feeling happy, or courageous, or compassionate, so that our actions will be in alignment with those feelings. If that's the case, we're all screwed when we wake up in a bad mood.

Imagine how different life would be if we shifted the order:

I am, therefore I do.

I do, therefore I feel.

In his book *Resilience*, author Eric Greitens writes, "When you put identity first—when you start from your conscious choice to be a certain kind of person—the way you think about achievement changes, too. You see that character precedes achievement."[2]

Yes! In other words, by focusing first on who you are, you then get to influence what you do and the results you create. I am, therefore I do. I do, therefore I feel. It's so much more empowering. That is the life order of a significance mindset.

Do you know any people who are truly dedicated runners? They run in the rain. They run in the snow. They run in the sun. With all due respect, these people are crazy.

Not me. I run when only I'm chased or trying to flag down an ice cream truck. Other than that, I'm totally content walking. My hamstrings remind me of that.

Runners run. They run on days even when they don't feel like running. Why do runners run? Because they're runners. That's what runners do.

If you have kids, like I do, you've experienced something similar. Do you remember waking up with your three-year-old every time he had to go to the bathroom in the middle of the night? Did you get up because you felt like leaving the warm coziness of your bed? Did you feel like tripping over the dog on the way to the bathroom, only to get blinded by the light that your son insisted on turning on? Did you feel like standing there, slightly delirious and praying that he wasn't peeing all over the toilet? If you're sane, you didn't feel like doing any of that.

But you did it anyway. When getting out of bed contradicted everything you felt like doing at that moment, why did you get up? Because you're a parent, and that's what good parents do.

Do you think a member of the U.S. Marine Corps feels like going into a building where the enemy awaits him? I'm not a marine so I can't speak first hand, but I have a hard time believing that they operate in those moments according to how they feel. I think there's a reason that "honor, courage and commitment" are driven into the identity and mindset of every marine. Why? Because in those moments of absolute chaos, every marine wants to believe that he can rely on the marine next to him to do what a marine does, even if he doesn't feel like doing it in that moment.

We do things even when we don't feel like it. Identity is the source.

BALLFUL MONTH

When I was a junior in high school, I was barely five feet tall and weighed a whopping one hundred and twenty pounds. I was a pale redheaded kid who struggled to stay upright in a strong wind, so you can imagine how unmarked my "date night" calendar looked.

I was also pretty shy when it came to asking girls out. I would stall, make excuses, and basically do everything I could to not ask someone out, then spend the next week stewing and hating myself for being so hesitant. It was a vicious cycle.

Luckily for me, my buddy, John, was similar. Not in stature, but in his shyness with girls. One day, we decided to do something about it.

We declared the following month, May, as Ballful Month. No need to look "ballful" up in the dictionary, by the way. You won't find it there. We made it up.

Ballful Month was the month where we would act like someone who had "balls." My apologies to the women reading this, but hey, we were teenagers. It was our month to forget how we felt about something and, instead, behave in a way where we could say, "Wow. That took some balls."

Our junior prom was scheduled for that month. For many kids, attending the junior prom is an exciting event, filled with tuxes and dresses, family pictures, travel arrangements, and planning how to get as drunk as possible without getting caught.

For John and me, our junior prom was different. I mean, we wanted to figure out the drinking part, but pretty much everything else about it was different than the typical experience.

John's relationship with his parents was... interesting. I'm not entirely sure I can even capture the essence of their relationship adequately. John's parents are wonderful people. They are also very old school. If John were to go to the prom, he needed to provide them with more information than, "Hey, I'm going with this girl, Sam. I'll be back at midnight."

His parents needed to meet Sam. For all they knew, she could have been Satan's daughter. Meeting Sam posed its own challenges since John wasn't allowed to have girlfriends until he reached the age of forty—at least that's how we interpreted what his parents expected of him. Sam wasn't even his official girlfriend, which would have opened up a whole new conversation about their friendship.

Additionally, they were going to want to know the exact details of the night's activities, like where the prom was being held, the time of the event, and the travel arrangements. Worst of all, they'd probably request that John get home by midnight.

All very reasonable requests, now that I reflect as a parent. However, from the eyes of a sixteen-year-old who just wanted to go out, get hammered, and stay at my house, this posed a tricky situation.

It was tricky because I wasn't attending my junior prom. I had broken my collarbone at wrestling practice a few weeks before the prom and my arm was still in a sling.

That's the reason I still prefer to use, anyway. The other reason is that I'm not sure I could have found a date.

Instead, my way to be involved in the prom was to host the "after-prom" party at my house. Were my parents cool with that, you ask? Hell no. Not even close. But they wouldn't know. They were going on vacation that weekend, and for some reason they thought it was a good idea to leave me home with my brother, Joe, who at the time was a senior in college.

Cha-ching!

The challenge was twofold: How could we get John to the prom without his parents knowing, and how could I host the huge open house without my parents finding out? The struggle was real.

There were plenty of times during the weeks leading up to the prom when our better judgments begged us to pay them some attention. The logistics of how John was going to tell his parents about spending the night at my house, rent a tux, bike to my house with the tux in hand (no licenses or cars yet, so it was a bike ride of one hour and thirty minutes), coordinate getting John to another friend's house for pictures, heading back to my house, host a party, and not get caught for any of it, was mind-boggling. Seems doable, right?

For days on end, John and I would discuss this seemingly impossible task. We contemplated if he should suck it up and tell his parents. That would alleviate one problem. We contemplated seeing if someone else could host the party, and maybe I could get Joe to drive me there to hang out. That would alleviate another problem.

We thought about calling the whole thing off. We weren't sure the risk was worth the reward. The scheming plans were getting complicated. The logistics were too unpredictable. To think about the consequences of things going wrong was unbearable. We knew, deep within our souls, that if we got caught for any of it, our lives would change in an abrupt, painful way at the hands of our parents.

Given our options, we did what any normal sixteen-year-old boys would do: We moved forward with our plan. Why? Because it was Ballful Month, dammit. This is what you do when you're participating in Ballful Month. You grow some balls.

On the day of reckoning, we set our plan in motion.

After trying to ride his bike while holding his tux, and subsequently almost crashing on a number of occasions, John decided to have a cab drive him (and his tux and bike) to my house. The limo picked him up there, and proceeded to pick up his date. Everyone came back to my house after the prom, and I parked the limos in my backyard. The following morning, I mowed the grass to erase the evidence of tire marks, dirtied the basement back to its normal look, and then waited for parental retribution. But it never came. Boo yah! It went off without a hitch.

During the months that followed our inaugural Ballful Month, life returned back to normal. I was still a scrawny little redheaded guy who lacked the confidence in many areas of my life.

Soon it was time for another Ballful Month.

Now in our senior year, John and I decided to increase the risk factor. Attending a prom and hosting a party seemed too easy, as if we could coordinate something so mischievous in our sleep. We needed to coordinate two separate events in one weekend and get away with it all.

Some fellow seniors had coordinated a scavenger hunt to take place on a random Friday night in October. That's all we needed to hear. We declared October as "Ballful Month II."

For those unfamiliar with a scavenger hunt, let me provide some details.

Imagine having a list of ten to twenty items. Each item, ranging from a Taco Bell flag to a wheelchair to an eight ball, had varying points assigned to it. Teams would be formed, consisting of three to eight people, depending on how many kids you could cram into one car, legally or illegally.

A designated timeframe with starting and stopping times was determined, typically something like 9:00 p.m. start and 11:00 p.m. finish. The team that successfully returned to the finish line with the most items valued with the most points was the winner. The winning prize was bragging rights, and maybe a few beers.

Because contestants didn't receive the itemized list of items until the official start time, there was no way to prepare in advance for the hunt. There was a certain strategy that went into the preparation, though. Who would be the driver? Whose car would we use? How many people could we fit with us? Lots of important decisions.

On the day of the scavenger hunt, we decided that John would drive, and we'd use his dad's 1979 Chevy Caprice Classic, with the emphasis on "Classic." It was a big car with a big trunk. Five of us formed a team. We were one team among twenty others.

The scavenger hunt started. We attacked the list ferociously. A street sign was an item with a hefty point value. We had the tools in the trunk, and shortly after, we had our sign. We successfully found, borrowed, perhaps stole a number of items on the list, and then we decided to get ourselves an eight ball.

Pulling up to a billiards hall, three of us volunteered to be the ones to leave with the eight ball. When we walked in, every set of eyes turned to look at us. It was clear that it was unusual for high school kids to show up at 10:30 p.m. to play pool. This was going to be tough.

None of us had any money, so we couldn't pay for a set of balls to play a game. Had that been possible, leaving with the eight ball, though still illegal, would have been easier.

The plan was for my buddy, Pat, to snatch a ball and hightail it out of there. Pat was the fastest runner of us all. He seemed like the obvious choice for the task. My job was to get John to pull around to the front of the hall and be ready to open the door for Pat when he came out. He was going to make a run for it.

With four of us waiting in John's running car, parked directly in front of the pool hall, Pat emerged in a flash.

The passenger door swung open. Pat dove into the back. We quickly closed the door and John peeled out. The Caprice's wheels screeched, as the patrons of the pool hall came pouring out chasing Pat. John stuck that gas pedal to the floor and we took off... for about one hundred feet, until we stopped at a red light.

Why John decided to be a law-abiding citizen in that exact moment is beyond me. There wasn't a car in sight. We begged the light to turn green, and waited for what seemed like an eternity. The light turned green, and we escaped unharmed.

Upon returning to the finish line of the scavenger hunt, with car after car emptying all of their "goods," it soon became clear we were not going to win.

After hearing all of the various stories from the other teams, we decided to end our night on a high note and leave the party. It was a good idea to leave when we did, since the sirens and lights of the police were just a short distance away.

We didn't win the scavenger hunt but we successfully completed the first leg of Ballful Month II. Next up: Party at John's house the next night.

The night after the scavenger hunt, John's parents were away for the night. Throwing a party while the parents were away, though still risky, seemed manageable after what we were able to pull off just a few months prior.

It wasn't so easy this time.

Arrangements were made in advance for John to spend the night at my house. We had to tell my parents we were going out (without providing too many details), head back to John's house to host the party, and then return back to my house to sleep.

The party started and quickly got out of hand. The kitchen freezer was raided, food was thrown everywhere, and people were doing ungodly things in every room in the house. As my curfew, and therefore ultimately John's curfew, quickly approached, I needed to return home. If I was late, my parents would be waiting up, ready to punish us both.

We faced multiple problems.

One, John's house was an absolute disaster.

Two, there were still people in his house. He couldn't leave yet.

Three, the curfew was fast approaching.

Four, I drove to the party. He didn't have a car, which meant that if I left he would have to bike over to my house in the early hours of the morning.

Five, we would have to hide the bike from my parents, who would wonder how the bike got to my house when it wasn't there the night before.

We decided that it was best for me to head home, on time, which I did. Being that my bedroom was on the ground level, I left my window open for John to climb through when he finally biked it back to my house.

When we awoke the next morning, both John and I felt good about accomplishing this minor feat. What we didn't realize was that things were about to get worse, quickly.

Sitting at the kitchen counter eating breakfast, my dad came over to ask us about our evening. We mumbled a few sentences, hoping that would be enough to quench his curiosity. It wasn't.

Resting his huge forearms on the counter, dad leaned in and said, "So, John, how was your party last night?"

I almost choked on my Frosted Flakes. There was a tense pause as both John and I raced for a plausible answer to that question. In a flash, our breakfast was our version of the Last Supper.

"Oh, it was good, Dr. Smith," John answered. Silence.

Flush with the satisfaction that he had caught us, my dad smiled. "Would you like to know how I know about the party?" he asked.

Is this a trick question? I couldn't tell.

"Sure," I said.

"Your friends kept calling last night, asking if you were at John's house. Then they asked me for directions to his house."

I could only shake my head. What was wrong with my friends?

Assured that the house was still standing and no one had gotten killed, my dad seemed content with his victory. After all, it wasn't his house that we absolutely destroyed.

When John returned home the next day, he had every intention of cleaning the house spotless and restocking the fridge and freezer, which had been decimated by aggressive party-goers the night before. Unfortunately for him, he didn't realize his parents would arrive home thirty minutes after his return.

Needless to say, it wasn't a "welcome home" greeting between John and his parents. From John's recollection, there were words spoken that would make a priest blush. John was grounded "until kingdom come" and he wasn't about to ask for clarity around the actual timeframe of what that meant.

The following day, the phone rang at John's house. It was the police. They had some questions about John's whereabouts on Friday night. It seems somebody had written down his license plate from the billiards hall and reported a stolen eight ball.

John's parents were irate. They couldn't believe John engaged in such mischievous behavior, and on consecutive nights, no less. They then grounded him "until kingdom come *and then some.*"

That Monday, the five of us who were together during the scavenger hunt had to find the eight ball that we had thrown out of the car and return it to the owner of the billiards hall. Somehow we managed to do this. I imagine the scene was quite comical through the eyes of the billiards hall owner, chastising five boys dressed in their catholic school uniforms for stealing an eight ball from his hall. Never once did he mention anything about being impressed with the speed with which we pulled it off, though. Some people are too shortsighted!

Needless to say, the great new tradition of Ballful Month came to an abrupt halt. We couldn't risk doing anything more that could result in being grounded for longer than "kingdom come and then some." This was our senior year, after all.

Ballful Month, as foolish as we were to create it, was a clear indicator that human behavior can be influenced by something more than our feelings. Our behavior can stem from our identity, who we are, and what we want to be about.

We did things during that month that clearly weren't guided by our feelings. We acted based on who we wanted to be that month. We wanted to be boys who had some "balls," who took risks, who lived life on the edge. We had an idea of who we wanted to be and acted accordingly.

I'm not trying to encourage mischievous or illegal activity. I'm not suggesting that you create your own version of "Ballful Month." I'm not discrediting the role of feelings, yours or some-one else's. This isn't about becoming a person who doesn't care about how others feel. That would make you a pretentious ass. Clearly, my friends and I could have shown a little restraint.

The point I'm making is that we can guide and even control how we feel more than we realize. If we can control our behavior, we can *create* how we feel.

If you want to feel happy, do something in accordance with someone who is happy. If you want to feel empowered, act empowered. If you want to feel compassionate, act with compas-sion. If you want to feel like your life is meaningful, act as if it's meaningful.

Identity. Actions. Feelings.

The question to consider, then, is this: "Whom do you need to be in order to do what you need to do, so that you feel how you want to feel?"

To answer that question, you'll need to first answer this one: "Who are you?"

DEATH BY ASSESSMENT

I'm aware that I can potentially upset many of my well-meaning friends who are certified to deliver various personality assessments. I accept that. But I'm going to say this anyway.

Here goes: *personality assessments are nonsense.*

Personality assessments place you in a box. For many people, being placed in a proverbial box is counter to what they believe about themselves, which is that they are unique.

These assessments give people permission they don't need and an excuse they conveniently use to act in a way that aligns with whatever box their assessment says they're in. I'm an individual, they say, except they're okay with being placed in a stereotypical box when it suits them.

People become giddy with this stuff. "OMG," they say. "This assessment analysis totally knows me." Of course it does. The answers you gave are probably in alignment with how you have chosen to act over the course of your life. Why is that so surprising?

Think about it. I like results. I have lived my life in a way that helps generate the results I want. Therefore, I'm going to choose the answer on an assessment questionnaire that most aligns with what my behavioral pattern has been previously. Then, it will spit out an answer that says my personality style is such where I am driven by results.

Not science. *Choice.*

I see this in management circles all the time. Here's an example.

A manager, let's say his name is Dave, takes an assessment and the results come back that his personality style is that of a "director." Let's not even discuss the validity of the findings due to how Dave may have answered those questions, which was according to how he felt someone in his position would be expected to answer the questions. I'll ignore that huge potential discrepancy.

Some analysis is going to talk about how Dave is a take-charge kind of person. He likes results. He can be demanding. He wants information and he wants it now. Get straight to the point with this type of person, the analysis says. No beating around the bush.

In fairness, it will probably state the shortcomings of this particular style, and therefore Dave, as well. It may state that he can be too demanding, perhaps not a great listener. He may need to be more diligent in hearing the opinions of others. The list goes on.

But here's where things get juicy. At home with his family, Dave's not like this at all. As a matter of fact, he's actually the exact opposite. His daughter schedules a "daddy date" and together they have a tea party with her dolls. His wife asks him what movie he wants to watch and he says, "Whatever you want to watch is fine with me." He's a smitten, huggable pushover. He's an aggressive cuddler. Not at all the demanding manager at work. What's the deal?

What these "scientifically proven" (questionable, by the way, to say they're scientifically proven) assessments fail to mention is that how you behave in any given situation still comes back to how you *choose* to behave at any given time.

Dave chooses to act like a director at work because that is how he has found success previously, or maybe it's how he believes one needs to act in order to be successful at work.

Dave chooses to have a tea party with his daughter at home because that is how he has found success in his relationship with her and he loves it.

Yes, it may be easy for you to act in a manner consistent with the analysis of whatever style you're assigned, but don't believe for a minute that you are acting that way outside of your choice or control.

Personality assessments aren't the only way we try to get some clarity around who we are.

Zodiac signs say people born at a specific time of the year have very specific tendencies, and people who behave in accordance with that synopsis believe in them.

Birth order is another classic assessment. The first born is controlling, cautious, and an achiever. The middle child is a somewhat rebellious peacemaker. The baby of the family is clearly spoiled, self-centered, fun loving, and manipulative.

It may be true that you or members of your family fit those descriptions. There are tons of exceptions, however. I'm the seventh of eight children in my family. Not too many studies done on that one. No one's ever says, "Oh, you're such the typical seventh child."

Garbage.

Because something comes easily does not mean it comes naturally. Too often we assume that if something requires little effort on our part, or if we find ourselves acting in a specific way consistently, it must be because we're genetically wired that way.

Not true.

Being cynical may come easily to you. Perhaps cynicism was modeled for you at home growing up. Maybe you've had plenty of bad breaks in your life and you've become jaded. But cynicism is not a natural way of being.

Being negative. Being a perfectionist. Being a procrastinator. All of these may come easily to you, but none of them come naturally.

People often dismiss their responsibility in choosing to be a certain way by saying, "It's just the way I am." No, it's just the way you're *choosing* to be.

Babies are not born with a perfectionist mindset. It's a learned behavior. You might be inclined to be a specific way, certainly. But that doesn't mean you need to be that way.

Despite your efforts to dye it for the past twenty years, your hair color comes naturally. Your height comes naturally. Your eye color comes naturally. Regardless of what you do, outside of anything superficially modified, you cannot change these things about yourself. They are what come naturally.

Neither your behavior nor your mindset falls into this category.

Again, not science. Choice.

THE POWER OF IDENTITY

Identity is about connection. It's about belonging, and the sense of belonging is one of the most basic and fundamental desires of a human being.

Human beings were never meant to be isolated. We're communal people. Not only do we get a sense of safety when we're members of a group, we can also recognize that our greatest moments of joy and happiness include other people.

When the New York Giants won the Super Bowl in 2008 and 2011, they weren't exactly the most dominant team in either season. Throughout the playoffs and into the final game, I chewed my nails down to the nubs because every game was close. Each game generated moments of extreme tension, excitement, and anxiety for me and for the fans of the opposing teams as well.

During the playoffs, I watched the games at a nearby bar with a group of friends. At the end of each game, with the Giants victorious, I ended up hugging people I'd never met. It didn't matter if he was a large three-hundred-pound bearded dude or a petite blonde girl. If they were wearing a Giants jersey, they were giving and receiving hugs. Why? Because we were all connected as Giants fans.

Identity by itself, when used as a means for connection, is beneficial. It's when identity is used to distinguish superiority or inferiority that it becomes divisive, dangerous, and even lethal.

Let's consider race for a minute. If someone says they are "color blind" (and I don't mean color blind due to genetics), they're lying. If we're honest with ourselves, we're actually very color conscious.

If you can't tell that I'm white or if someone else is black, or Asian, something is wrong with your eyesight. How are we to experience the beauty of our individuality if we refuse to acknowledge that we are different?

But by "different" I do not mean "better" or "worse." I do not mean "superior" or "inferior."

Some of my friends are white. Some are black. Some are Asian. Some are brunette. Some are blonde. Some have red hair (those are my favorites, because God made us totally superior in that sense)!

Can we stop trying to pretend we don't recognize our differences? We do, and we should. What we should stop is trying to figure out how people just like me are better than those who are not.

Consider the different identities you possess. Think of your last name. What does it mean to be a _____ (fill in your last name)? I'm a Smith, and the Smiths are fun, family-oriented, tough, athletic, compassionate people. That's who we are, from my perspective.

I can even break it down into my personal identity. I am a Smith. I am a Christian. I am a husband, a father, a brother, an uncle. I am a wrestler. I am a speaker. I am an author. I could continue, but you get the point.

Your identities may be similar or different. You might say, I am a product of a broken home. I am an alcoholic. I am an alienated parent. I am a go-getter. I am in sales. I am an architect. I am a CEO. I am a mom. I am a dad.

You might also notice that we categorize ourselves into our personal identities, as outlined above, or in a group identity. Perhaps you consider your identity as being connected to the company you work for. Maybe your identity is attached to something more status related, such as I am rich or I am poor.

The power of our identities isn't necessarily in *what* we align ourselves to, but rather the *meaning* we assign to that identity. In other words, it's what we make our identity mean that drives our behavior. We are inclined to act in accordance with how we view ourselves, regardless of whether our views are accurate or not.

Our identity of self is what contributes to our intrinsic motivation. I mentioned before that I consider myself to be athletic. Let's be clear. I'm no Olympic athlete. But by considering myself a decent athlete, what's important is not that I like to play softball, or golf, or soccer. What's important is that I was more inclined to *start* playing those sports because I *already* considered myself a good athlete. For some reason I had confidence that I could learn a particular sport and play in an adequate manner. There's also a sense of satisfaction that derives from behaving in accordance with who I believe I am.

I talked about the crazy runners previously. I say "crazy" as a term of endearment. I'm secretly just jealous of them. I mentioned that runners run because that's what runners do. Being a runner has become such a part of their identity that it almost seems unnatural for them not to run.

You see in the previous examples of how identity can lead to something positive. It's also what tends to hold people back. Those who identify themselves as "not smart" might minimize their potential and not pursue something because they don't think they have the intellect to succeed.

A person who has struggled with an illness, or who has been taking medication for as long as they can remember, may begin to view themselves as someone who is sick. Once that mindset of being a sick person has set in, they may deem themselves ineligible for certain activities because it's not something that "a sick person" would do. Certainly, there may be things they cannot do, but there could be a margin of things they could possibly do, if they were open to it.

I had a stroke. I fully recovered, and for that I am grateful. But even in that I can distinguish what it means regarding my identity. I could just as easily describe myself as a stroke "victim" as I could a stroke "survivor." I can also choose neither of those terms and, instead, simply state that I had a stroke. The choice is mine.

This is why gaining a good understanding of ourselves is so critical to living in a significant way. While we might be our own greatest asset, we could also be our own greatest limitation. You can't expect your behavior to change if it's contradictory to what you generally believe about who you are.

The good news is that we get to choose who we want to be. Yes, genetics play a role, but our choice can be a stronger influence. Choose first. Choose who you want to be, choose what you want to stand for, and then act accordingly.

Choose to be a loving wife.

Choose to be a faithful husband.

Choose to be a valued employee.

Choose to be outgoing and friendly.

Choose. Choose. Choose.

YOUR CORE WORDS

As was the case with the words "I choose," there is something empowering about using the words "I am."

Too many people spend their days trying to act one way at work and another way at home. To me, that's exhausting. The business community often promotes this idea that we should be able to keep our personal life separate from our professional life. That sounds great, except for one minor detail: I have yet to meet one person that can actually do that well.

We're kidding ourselves if we think that circumstances in our homes don't affect us at work, just as much as things that happen to us at work affect us at home.

Do you know what it's like to get young kids out the door when you're expected to be somewhere at a designated time? Parenting is waking up two hours earlier than you want to and arriving two hours later than you were supposed to. It's incomprehensible.

It's easy to bring to work the stress of getting the kids ready in the morning and driving through rush hour traffic. Then later, it's common to bring frustration at work home in the evening.

I'm not saying we shouldn't proactively manage the stress in one environment so that it doesn't negatively create more stress in the other environment. Of course we should. Rather, I'm referring more to who we are as individuals in each aspect of our lives.

Imagine how freeing it would be to say, "This is who I am," and then being that person in every facet of your life. Not only is it possible, I think this is exactly how we were meant to live.

By being who you truly are, you're more inclined to make a difference in this world. The more you hide, the less your impact. If you're to live more fully into who you are as an individual, then you need to gain some clarity around who you are. As I mentioned previously, the answer won't be found in some personality assessment. It's found in who you choose to be.

Let's do a simple exercise. Spend a few seconds writing down at least ten words you would use to describe you at your best and that you know to be true about yourself.

Now, chop that list in half by underlining five of your favorite words.

Finally, circle the top three words which resonate with you the most, the ones that totally embody everything you want to be.

Don't spend a lot of time completing this exercise because then you'll start to overanalyze it. You know who you are.

See those three words on your paper? Today's goal is for you to *be* those three words the entire day, both at work and at home. Print them. Post them. Be them.

I can find out more about you by knowing those three words than by reading a synopsis of your personality profile. They reveal the best parts of you, as defined by you. You can't ask for a higher level of ownership than that.

DON'T FAKE IT, BECOME IT

The three words you've selected can be words to describe how you currently are or who you aspire to become.

If you want to become more patient but currently struggle with that, you can use "patience" as one of your three words to signify who you want to become. Does that mean you're faking it, that somehow you're inauthentic, or pretending to be a certain way when, in fact, you're not?

Yes and no.

I mentioned previously that I am a wrestler. In the wrestling community, we often talk about how being a wrestler is a way of life. The sport shifts your mindset, your values, and your determination in ways that influence a person both personally and professionally.

But at what point did I become a wrestler? Was it when I stepped on the mat for the first time at the age of six? Did lacing up my shoes for the first practice or match make me a wrestler? Did I need to compete through college, as I did, to consider myself a wrestler?

No. I became a wrestler when I chose to incorporate being a wrestler into who I am. In other words, I became a wrestler when I chose to be a wrestler. Every day, I decide what I want "being a wrestler" to mean and I choose whether or not to incorporate that into my identity. My choice.

Though I've played softball for years, I do not identify myself as a softball player. For one, I don't even know what that means because I haven't assigned a meaning to it. What does it mean to be a softball player? I have no idea.

Therefore, I say that I *play* softball, while I say I *am* a wrestler.

My dad, on the other hand, might call himself a softball player. He played for the better part of fifty years, and his stellar career resulted in his election to the National Softball Hall of Fame. Being that good of a softball player may lead him to incorporate that into his identity. It's up to him.

This isn't a matter of semantics. There is a huge difference between identifying ourselves by the use of the words "I am..." and using words such as "I play..." One relates to an identity. The other references an activity.

Consider, also, exactly *when* you became the person you say you are. When does someone say they are a patient person? Do they have to wait to act patiently until they can claim that as being a part of their identity? Or, can they state that being patient is who they are, and then live in to that way of being accordingly?

If you're trying to live as if you already are what you want to become, you may feel like you're faking it to some extent. But if we had to wait until something happened for us to then say we are a certain way, how would we ever work toward developing ourselves into a better person?

Acting your way into being can be empowering if you are trying to incorporate a way of being that benefits you. Act courageous to become more courageous. Act compassionate to become more compassionate.

This is not my blessing for the "fake it 'till you make it" mantra. I think that phrase is overused and misunderstood, often in the business community.

I frequently hear people advise young managers to "fake it 'till you make it." Some of them interpret that as an instruction to act as if they know the answers and they have it under control. No wonder they struggle with this.

Imagine this type of thinking in your marriage. Try faking being loyal until you become loyal. Good luck getting that concept past your significant other. I hope you have a good divorce attorney.

Acting in ways in which you know are either inauthentic or even contradictory to what you know to be true about yourself is fraudulent. It's a mask, a front, and a charade. People will see through that crap quickly, and you run the risk of being considered a hypocrite.

This isn't a matter of faking who you are for the sake of pleasing someone else. This is a choice to become the person you strive to be. Don't fake it; become it.

YOUR CORE STAND

Deciding who you are is critical to living in a significant way. Now I want you consider what you want your life to be about. What's your stand? What do you stand for?

Your stand is what drives you. Your stand is what motivates you. Your stand is what gives your life meaning.

I'm not talking about passion. I love passion. It's just that passion is a feeling, and as we know, feelings come and go. Passion, when we feel it, is awesome.

But what happens in those moments when we don't feel passionate?

Instead, what I'm talking about is something much more powerful and sustainable than passion. What I'm referring to is your *purpose*.

A discussion on purpose doesn't have to be some deep, spiritually insightful, tear-filled conversation. We don't need to light incense, turn down the lights, or start talking about feelings. Of course, you can if you want to, but I don't think it's necessary.

Some people find the idea of their life meaning as elusive as the Loch Ness monster. We often hear about how people are trying to find their purpose, with some spending their entire lives seeking but never finding it. Those who spend their time searching that way are operating under a false assumption.

In order to find something, we must assume that it is lost, hidden, or out of site.

Your purpose is none of those things.

Your purpose is something you choose. Beyond your choice, you create it. You control what you want your life to be about because it's simply a matter of choice. Your choice.

You may think that it can't be so simple and that there must be more to it than that. There's not. We make it more difficult than it needs to be. Perhaps you're more content to stay searching, fearing that if you were to actually choose your purpose, you would then be prompted to act.

Granted, there are events in our lives that may pique our interest or emotions in ways never before experienced. The mistake, however, is assuming that a specific event is what led us to act on a life purpose. Not entirely. An event presents a certain set of circumstances, which we then get to make choices around. An event is just an event. What makes an event impactful is the meaning we assign to it and the choices we make around it.

Like me, there have been plenty of people who have had a stroke in their lifetimes. Some may have used that as a defining moment in their lives. Others may happen to mention it in no different a tone than telling someone they ate eggs for breakfast. I choose to make my stroke what it was for me: a life changing moment that has been a springboard to help deliver the message that we are created to live a life of significance.

What's your stand? What are those one or two words that embody the totality of you? Is it "faith," or "love," or "family," or "commitment," or "integrity," or some other word that gets you energized just thinking about it?

I stand for "significance" and "impact." Those two words mean something to me. They resonate most with me. When I think about how I want to be known, both now and in the future, it's as a person who made a significant impact in the lives of others and encouraged others to do the same.

Choosing your stand is the first step.

Living your stand is the next.

The beauty of choosing and living your stand is that this is your "Why" as well as your "What." Your stand is the reason why you do something, with the intent on generating results aligned with what you want to produce.

As I look at my personal life, because I stand for significance and impact, that's what drives me to figure out how I can be a better dad to my kids. I proactively look for ways to improve myself for their betterment.

My stand, then, alters my behavior as it relates to my boys. One way is through my work schedule. On most days, I have the pleasure of dropping them off at school, which means I try not to schedule a work responsibility before 9:00 a.m. I also enjoy picking them up from school, which means I try not to schedule anything past 4:30 p.m.

I'm willing to make sacrifices, if you can even consider that example a sacrifice, because what I hope to create is a significant difference in their lives. I don't mind the sacrifice because the reward is so much greater. If I'm able to make a significant impact in the lives of kids, then any sacrifice required to make that happen is worthwhile.

As I look at my professional life, my stand is what drives me to create presentations and programs that will make a difference in people's lives. This book is a great example. Before I ever jotted a word down on paper, my initial thought was, "What could I possibly say to anyone who reads it that might make a difference in his or her life?"

The words in this book are written with the intent to change your life. That is a bold and monumental task. Will I hit the mark with some of you? Heck, yes! Will I fall short with others? Possibly. But what's the alternative? To play it safe? To write a bunch of words that make people feel good but don't drive to the heart of what matters most? I won't do that because it's not who I am and it's not what I stand for.

To me, it's worth the risk to write the really difficult thing, even if that means upsetting some people along the way. I choose to remain true to who I am and the message I want to deliver. I know there are people who are reading this book at the perfect time of their lives. Perhaps for the past few months or even years you've been considering what I'm referring to. Maybe you know that you were called for something more than what you're currently doing. Maybe this is the wake-up call that you needed.

Businesses that stand for something begin to attract and relate to their customers in ways never before experienced. Teams that take a stand strengthen their commitment, both to each other and those they serve, because taking a stand creates a foundation of trust. Trust is developed not through what we consider to be someone else's predictability but through their *consistency*. Decision-making becomes easier, even in the most difficult of situations, if we can revert back to that which we have declared as our stand.

Individuals who take a stand also stand out among the rest. They are purpose-driven. They are mission-driven. They are living in a way that fulfills their desire to know with certainty that who they are and what they do matters.

ACCEPT THE RISK

George Washington took a stand when he willingly, and without hesitation, relinquished his power and title of the presidency when there was no precedent to follow. In rejecting power, General Washington became the first modern military leader to win a war and not use it to seize power and control for himself.

Martin Luther King, Jr. took a stand for equality and fairness, even in the face of danger and rejection.

The restaurant chain Chick-fil-A takes a stand by not being open on Sundays, even though that happens to be the day I most crave their sandwiches and shakes.

Again I ask, what is your stand? Are you willing to draw a line in the sand and boldly declare, regardless of what others say, whether they agree or disagree, that this is what you choose your life to be about?

Does being so boldly self-expressive come at a risk? It can. Why? Because there are plenty of people who will willingly tell you, from their perspective, who you "should" be, what you "should" do, how you "should" think. Then, you'll begin to realize how you've been "should" on your entire life. Stop being "should" on!

Equally as important as taking a stand *for* something is the absolute necessity of deciding what you will *reject*.

Remember that you control only your choices, not other people. While understandable, to decide that you will no longer stand to be treated disrespectfully is to assert you can control how other people interact with you. Instead, you may want to consider that you will no longer interact with people who mistreat you, or you will no longer allow their interaction with you to affect you in negative ways.

I also want you to consider what you will reject within yourself. Declare that you will no longer allow yourself to be a victim.

Declare that you will no longer be negative. Declare that you will no longer be held back by your insecurities. There are plenty of obstacles in this life that have the potential to hold us back. Declare that your own issues won't be one of them.

Make today the day that you choose what you want your life to be about. Determine what you will and will not stand for anymore.

Take a stand.

5

POKE THE LION

"The greatest fear in the world is the opinion of others, and the moment you are unafraid of the crowd, you are no longer a sheep, you become a lion. A great roar arises in your heart, the roar of freedom."

~ Osho

Do you remember playing tag as a kid? For me, it came with conditions. I loved playing when I knew I was faster than the others who were playing. I didn't enjoy it nearly as much if I knew I could get caught at any moment. It wasn't as fun being "it" as it was running and hiding from "it."

I remember playing with a friend of mine. While I was vertically challenged, O.C. was vertically blessed. O.C. and I would play tag with other friends for hours. One game, I was about fifty yards away from the person designated as "it." Somehow, "it" caught O.C., who then became "it."

I assumed that O.C. would run to one of the boys closest to him in order to tag him. He didn't. Instead, O.C. was like a meerkat, those little animals that stretch up on their back legs to scope out the landscape.

I knew for whom he was looking.

Because O.C. was so tall, it was easy for him to search the entire playing area. Unfortunately, having red hair doesn't exactly help you blend into your environment, unless you're hiding in a strawberry patch. It was pretty much a foregone conclusion that he was going to find me.

Our eyes locked, and devilish grins came across our faces. The hunt was on. This was our National Geographic moment. I swear I even saw O.C. lick his lips.

When I was younger, I was fast. But I wasn't as fast as O.C. If I was a gazelle, O.C. was a cheetah. I knew he'd gain ground eventually. In a flash, I took off running.

My heart was pounding as I ran away from O.C. After just a few short strides, I could already hear his powerful legs behind me. Then, I could hear him breathing. I knew he was close.

I don't do well when chased. The uncertainty of when I was going to get caught became unbearable for me. I decided to turn and face him. He was too close. I couldn't maneuver around him, as I had done at times before. I was tagged. I became "it" and it was my turn to chase the other boys. Off I went, running as fast as I could to tag someone else, and we continued to play for hours.

I tell this story because I think fear operates in a very similar way in our lives. The more we turn and run from it, the tighter the grip, whether real or imagined, it has on us. If there's one thing that acts as both a springboard and a ceiling for our success, it's the internal fears, self-doubts and insecurities we deal with every day.

When fear beats you down, you must turn and face it.

WHAT ARE WE SO AFRAID OF?

Let's have a candid conversation about our fears. We all have them, as much as we never really talk about them. Maybe we believe that by exposing our fears, people might view us as weak. Some may believe that we should not expose our fears and that other leaders will prey on those fears. To them, it's all about appearing strong.

It seems to me that *acknowledging* the fear without *glorifying* the fear normalizes it. I've witnessed tremendous paradigm shifts in individuals and teams who incorporate the virtue of honesty into their daily communication. Defensive walls established by internal egos have crumbled in seconds when people choose to finally get real with each other.

Acknowledging the fear is not creating something that doesn't already exist. Fear has been with us all along. It's up to us to put it in its rightful place.

I don't know how many fears or which fears are inherent to us as humans. But we definitely all have internal fears. We have the ability to manifest fear into a legitimate internal obstacle that prevents us from moving forward in many aspects of our lives. But we also possess the ability to become its master.

I once worked with a client whom I'll call Stacy. When Stacy and I started working together, she was a new manager, eager to perform well in her new role as she had done in her previous role. However, shortly after her promotion, there was a noticeable difference in Stacy. She seemed on-edge, more stressed, more impatient. Her manager recognized it. Her co-workers recognized it. They asked me to help her out.

It's not uncommon for a college graduate to have a fear about whether she's going to get employed, which Stacy most certainly had. She feared that her resume wasn't strong enough to even be considered initially, which it was. She feared that she wouldn't interview effectively and get offered a position, which she did. Then she got hired, and she feared she wouldn't do a good job in her new role. Again, she did.

As a matter of fact, she performed so well that her upper management promoted her to be the manager of the team she was on. For many people, this is a great professional achievement, recognition of their hard work and excellent productivity.

Though Stacy felt honored to get the promotion, she was also consumed with an entirely new fear: the fear of being found out. The fear that she was a total fraud.

Think about the progression of her fears this way. At first, the fear was, "Will I get hired?" Then it progressed to, "Will I do a good job?" Then, upon the promotion, the fear became, "Holy crap! I'm not nearly as good as they think I am."

Think about the mindset of someone like Stacy, someone who has a fear of being a fraud or a fear of being found out. Every day while heading into work, in the back of her mind is the voice of the internal critic. This voice asks: "Is this the day I get asked a question that I don't know the answer to? And by not knowing the answer, will that open the eyes of someone else who will wonder why I hold the position I hold, because people with a position at this level should know the answers to these types of questions?"

At its most raw level, those who have a fear of being a fraud are in a heightened state of caution, wondering if the next moment, the next question, the next conversation will lead to someone recognizing that they have no idea what they're doing.

Think about how that influences someone's behavior. On Friday, Stacy was an employee. On Monday, she was a manager. Other than living through Saturday and Sunday, what changed for her? Well, nothing... except everything.

Stacy started making up answers to questions she didn't know. She grew more impatient with her co-workers, who were now her direct reports. What were once great relationships between them were now becoming strained with tension. She was successful as an employee but was now struggling as a manager. Throughout the entire process, she never really believed that she deserved to be at the level she was. She was running from what she feared most by putting as much distance between herself and others as possible.

Here's the thing—her fears were not serving her. Fear can be a great motivator. It's not a sustainable motivator, however. The longer someone continues to be driven by fear, the more likely they are to experience greater levels of frustration, increased irritation, and less personal and professional fulfillment.

It's time to address the fears, self-doubts and insecurities that we all possess. To do that, we need to focus on three things:

1. Our perspective about the fears in our life.

2. The importance of being persistent when facing our fears.

3. The crucial role that people play in our continued success.

PERSPECTIVE

In order for you to move beyond your fears, let's first develop the right context about them. When you understand the nature of your fear, you'll gain an appreciation of it. You'll recognize three important things: First, most of your fear has been created by you. Second, your fear is an internal mechanism designed to protect you from harm, perceived or real, present or future-based. Third, your fear demands an action.

You create your fears to protect you, and that's not entirely a bad thing. A healthy dose of fear is why homeowners invest in alarm systems. Fear is why we wear seat belts. Fear of a negative consequence is why you take the steak knives away from your boys as they try to cut Play-doh.

If there's something that doesn't feel right in your gut, take heed. If something doesn't look right, it may not be. There's nothing wrong with operating with caution at times. I think we're gifted with an innate sense of preservation.

There are also some common fears of snakes, or heights, or in my case, spiders. Put a big spider in front of me, and I'll knock down my own kids to get out of the way. Embarrassing, but true. But these aren't the fears that typically hold us back.

The fears that hold us back are the fears we don't talk about and the fears we don't typically share with other people. These are the fears which are influencing—possibly driving—our activity, or more likely, our inactivity.

The fears that hold us back aren't concerned about our physical safety. The focus isn't on protecting ourselves from bodily harm. They're focused on protecting what is often the most fragile component of a human being: the ego.

People are more likely to die from a fear of failure than a fear of poisonous snakes. People die from snake bites every year, yet this number pales in comparison to those who die trying to protect their ego, figuratively speaking. They die because they become a hollow shell of a person, choosing to never experience what it was like to actually live.

The fear of incompetence. The fear of looking foolish. The fear of being disliked. The fear of being a disappointment. The fear of abandonment or rejection. The fear of public speaking. The fear of losing out. The fear of missing out. The fear of losing your independence. The fear of being found out. The fear of being a fraud.

These are the fears that have successfully crushed more goals, dreams, and desires than one could possibly count. These are the fears that have ruined relationships, bankrupted our resolve, and seductively enticed people to live in complacency.

The most common fear I hear people mention is the fear of failure. This is a safe revelation and one that's easy to share with others because it's likely they'll nod their heads in agreement. They probably have the same fear. It's also the one I don't allow to stand by itself.

No one enjoys failure. There are plenty of people who say super-fluffy things like "embrace your failure" and how much their failure has led them to success. While I totally agree with the latter part of that sentence, let's not give off some fictitious illusion that most people dream about failing. Personally, I despise it; and yes, I've become successful because I've experienced it.

There's more to the fear of failure, though. Go deeper and ask yourself this question: What are you making "failure" mean about you? The answer to that question will reveal the underlying fear.

For some, failing is symbolic of not being smart enough, or tall enough, or charismatic enough. Perhaps failing means that you'd have to hear "I told you so" by some naysayer along the way. Maybe failing means you're simply not as good as you think you are.

What you'll notice about all of these fears is that they share a common root cause: The belief that "I am not enough." The thought of not being enough is enough to keep even the most confident person stationary from time to time.

The logical and traditional motivational next step would be for me to tell you that you are enough. You are strong enough. You are smart enough. You can figure this out. But I'm not going to tell you that because, honestly, I'm not sure it's true.

It's not up to me to superficially tell you what you are. I can merely talk about what we all possess. I do believe you possess the ability to become stronger and to become smarter. I even believe that you, like all of us, are enough. But what will make a difference in your life isn't who I believe you are or what I think you're capable of becoming. What will make a difference depends on what you choose to do about it.

If the root cause of our fear is that somehow we're not enough, the condemning weapon we constantly avoid is the judgment of others.

We know two things about judgment. First, no one likes to be judged by someone else. Second, we judge ourselves and others all the time.

Oh, the idea of being judgmental doesn't sit well with anyone, of course. No one wants to admit to being a person who judges others. Yet we do. What do we think a "first impression" is all about? A snap judgment.

Sadly, the reality is that your fear of being judged is based in reality. You will be judged. Believing anything contrary is borderline delusional and unhealthy. Therefore, it's not a matter of trying to convince yourself that you're not being judged, as much as it's important for you to gain a better perspective on whose opinion actually matters. It means more to me that my wife likes me than the random acquaintance I barely know.

There are critics in this world. There are cynics. There are those who get giddy at the thought of analyzing how you did everything wrong and why you were such a fool to even attempt to dare greatly. Their worth is attached to their belief that "they were right." They don't consider themselves as judgmental people, but they are. Sadly, they're now judgmental and ignorant.

Let us not also pretend that each of us is somehow more enlightened or better than anyone else. If we are honest with ourselves, there are times our thoughts are critiquing the activities of others. Not sure about that? The next time you hear yourself saying what someone should do or should have done, that's a judgment.

I mention this not so that we beat ourselves up over it, but as a way to become more aware of our own judgments. Typically, people are afraid of being judged on the very things they judge in others. It's human nature to have those judgmental thoughts. But it doesn't mean we need to keep them.

Those who worry about their weight judge the weight of others. Those who worry about their parenting choices judge the choices of other parents. And on and on.

As a speaker, I used to be critical of others who spoke. The temptation was to find what someone else didn't do well so that I could feel better about myself. It's not easy to admit something like that, but it was true for me at one time.

Once I realized this, I didn't want to do it anymore. I wanted to change. Knowing this about myself and being honest about it allowed me to stop those critiquing thoughts the moment I became aware of them.

I actively chose to notice something different about the person. I started identifying things the speaker did I thought were awesome. I watched their body movements while speaking and the way in which they weaved stories into their presentation. I listened to how they began their presentation and how they concluded it. I looked for ways to elevate my own performance by learning from anyone who was willing to stand in front of a crowd and speak.

It was such a slight but important shift in my thinking. I became a student instead of a critic. I proactively looked to surround myself with speakers who were absolutely crushing it on stage. By changing myself, I changed how I saw others. It was such a different experience to be intentional about finding the good.

There's more to judgment than being judged by someone else or judging someone else. We can, at times, do this especially well to ourselves. Sometimes your own worst critic stares back at you in the mirror every day.

Sometimes our fear can be a bit narcissistic. Have you ever worried that people at a party are talking negatively about you? Perhaps in isolated situations they are, but most of the time they're not. To think that others are spending their time thinking about you is, well, giving yourself too much credit. You're not nearly as important to them as you might imagine.

Clearly I'm poking fun at the topic. You aren't the topic of their conversations nearly as much as you think you are. Why? Because most people have their own internal issues to worry about. For many people, what they like to think and talk about mostly are themselves.

Sorry. You didn't make the cut.

Fear is a powerful entity in our lives. We choose what to do with it. It moves us to action and can also keep us chained with inaction. It creates worry, which is sometimes beneficial and sometimes limiting. We fear being judged yet one thing we know with certainty is that the world is full of people who will judge us. We judge others, which is typically a reflection of the things we most fear being judged about ourselves. We judge ourselves, often acting as our biggest critic and the one who holds us back most frequently.

The bottom line is that our fears, self-doubts, and insecurities require our awareness of their existence, and it's our responsibility to choose how we allow them to influence our lives.

Over time, a caged lion forgets it's a lion because it's been limited and defeated for so long. It's time to poke the lion.

You, my friend, are the lion.

PERSISTENCE

As hard as you might try, you can't deceive yourself. If your own fear is truly something you want to conquer, then prepare yourself mentally for a battle. Little that is meaningful is ever achieved easily.

You may never get to a point when all of your fears are decimated. New opportunities will inevitably bring about new impulses to protect yourself. Being persistent with your fears requires that you understand this is a life-long battle that can only be won a situation at a time.

When I was a wrestling coach, it wasn't too uncommon for a wrestler to speak to me about his desire to quit. Sometimes this was a conversation that occurred before the start of the season. Sometimes it occurred during the season.

The common excuse was typically something to the effect of wanting to focus on grades. I am a big believer that grades are important. If I thought their participation in wrestling was hindering their ability to achieve academic success, I'd be the first person to suggest they stop.

That was rarely the case.

Once I was able to get beneath the surface, the most common reason why a wrestler wanted to quit was simple: he just didn't want to commit to the sacrifice, discipline and hard work necessary to compete. I totally understood this, as I was someone who almost quit the sport between my first and second year in college. Thankfully, I stuck it out.

In that type of conversation, my first goal was to get the athlete to face their fear directly, to get him to admit the true reason for his desire to quit. Using his grades was an excuse that seemed to present a plausible reason that wouldn't garner any counter arguments. Who could argue with the importance of getting good grades?

Once he finally admitted his true fear, whatever it may have been, it was easier to address the situation through a different perspective. We could dissect his fear at a logistical and emotional level. Eventually we could talk about next steps, which was my second goal in the conversation.

I found I was most successful in those conversations when I didn't focus on everything the wrestler could achieve throughout the year. While I may have believed he was capable of much success, I would reserve that for a different conversation. Instead, when confronting the possibility of having him quit, my goal was to get him to agree to do something simple: show up to practice the next day.

Just show up. Act, do, feel.

With every day he showed up, the more committed he became, until the thought of quitting was no longer something he considered. One day at a time. I knew he was re-committed when I would say, "See you tomorrow," and he'd nod his head in agreement.

Athletes who consider quitting their sport but decide against it will often talk about how glad they are that they didn't quit. They realize they came to appreciate the grind and the struggle. They recognize how it made them a stronger individual. You can apply the same principle to your own life, in your business, personal situation—whatever it may be. Show up. Day after day.

Conquering your fears will require the same discipline and a "one day at a time" approach, primarily because the desire to quit may be fueled by the likelihood of your failed initial attempts at success.

The stronger the fear, the longer it may take to overcome it. Initially you may experience multiple setbacks, but there is a huge difference between someone who "failed" and someone who considers themselves "a failure."

Instead of saying "I will no longer have a fear of looking incompetent," say, "I will not let my fear of looking incompetent minimize me today." Just today. Tomorrow will present its own challenges. When tomorrow comes, begin with the same statement that keeps you focused on the twenty-four hours ahead of you.

Tom Brady, the quarterback for the New England Patriots, has won over two hundred career games. He is the all-time pro football leader in wins. At press conferences both he and his coach, Bill Belichick, are famously taciturn. To almost any question posed by a member of the press, Brady will inevitably respond, "We're only focused on the next game." Same with Belichik: "We're focused on the next game." Their reserve drives reporters crazy, but you know what? Brady and Belichick are telling the truth. The only thing they think about is the next game. Not the game next month or the one yesterday. Only the next game.

Persistence isn't just related to what you intend to do or what you think you might want to do. It's also important that you actually do things consistently that will help you conquer your fears. W. Clement Stone said, "Thinking will not overcome fear, but action will."

Teams and athletes practice certain drills every day, doing them so often they can execute them reflexively, without thinking. And that's exactly the purpose of repetition. You drill certain moves over and over again so that in the heat of the battle you're operating on instinct and muscle memory.

Not only do teams run through the same drills on a daily basis, they also put the players in positions they may likely find themselves on game day. In football, teams will practice the two-minute drill. In hockey, teams will practice their power play scenarios. In basketball, coaches may have the team practice the "five-seconds-remaining-and-we're-down-by-one" play.

Why prepare them in this way? Because they're more likely to perform at a higher level in situations they experienced previously, even in a manufactured atmosphere. Teams need this repetition because it creates a specific way of doing something, even when the opponent changes.

Coaches train their teams by putting them in positions they may be in during the game. They train them to do something that will help them become victorious.

While there is a time to reflect on what could be done better in the future, if they haven't prepared for when they're actually in that position, they will most likely fail to score. If they haven't prepared previously, it will be difficult for them to act in a way that will lead to victory presently.

Addressing your fears requires a similar commitment to go through the drills daily. Break each fear down into smaller parts and attack each one. Train your brain and body to respond in a way that suits you best.

This is more difficult to do than we realize. Because it requires us to realize our fear and then figure out how to face it. Our natural default reaction is to protect ourselves by feeding fear so we don't have to face it. This makes things worse.

Let me give you an example.

Take the fear of being disliked. No one intentionally sets out to be disliked by others. Quite the contrary, being liked is sometimes synonymous with being accepted, and acceptance by others is a deep desire shared by all.

But look at what this fear can do. The drive to be accepted and liked, as with many of our fears, can become a negative influence when taken to extremes. For those who fear being disliked, the tendency is for them to become "yes" people. By itself, there's nothing wrong with being an accommodating person, driven by the desire to please others. But taken to an extreme, not being able to say "no" leads to undue hardship.

Consumed with too many things to be responsible for generates feelings of irritation, frustration, and a sense of being overwhelmed. A person's attitude changes. Their behavior changes. They become "snappy" with others. They may begin to feel under-appreciated, often citing how much they do and how little they are recognized for their efforts.

They work longer hours. They accept more work. They say "yes" to being everything to everyone. Eventually, they burn out because their motivation was rooted in their fear of being disliked. It wasn't their purpose they so eagerly pursued. It was their fragile ego they wanted to protect.

The same fear of being disliked can wreak havoc on a manager. Take a manager who needs to make a decision regarding the direction of the team. Employee A has suggested his thoughts on what the team should do next. Employee B has also expressed her thoughts, and she believes the team should do the opposite of what employee A believes.

If the manager sides with employee A, he will most assuredly upset employee B. The opposite is also true. Feeling like there's no good solution and that he's screwed either way, what decision does the manager make? No decision, which now infuriates both employee A and B.

The manager who feared upsetting one employee has now upset both, which further triggers his fear of being disliked.

Same fear. Different situations.

The fear of being a disappointment is similar. When a new college graduate enters the workforce, they may have a fear of being a disappointment to mom and dad. Perhaps that's why they chose the school they attended. It may not have been their first pick but it was mom and dad's preference. That was enough for them to attend.

They may have received a degree in a program that they don't care about, mainly because mom or dad told them to get a degree that presented the most likely case for employment. From their parent's perspective, that was the smart thing to do.

When they become employed, the fear of disappointment gets expanded. They didn't want to disappoint mom and dad, and now they don't want to disappoint their manager.

When they get married and have kids, they may begin to fear being a disappointment to their parents again, this time with how they raise their children. They may wonder if mom and dad will approve their child rearing approach.

As their kids get older, they won't want to disappoint them as a parent. They may be paralyzed in those moments when they want to discipline a child but won't out of fear, for that would mean they are failing as a parent.

Again, the cycle continues. Same fear. Different situations.

Addressing the fear at such crucial moments in your life is much more challenging if you haven't already addressed that same fear in the multitude of smaller opportunities earlier.

Recognize those moments when a fear is triggered. Choose to act in a way that supports your stand. Will you stumble initially? Possibly. Facing, addressing, and conquering the fear was never about absolute certainty. It was always about focusing on the process to generate different results. It requires persistence.

PEOPLE

We learn by imitating what we see, hear and believe. There is no greater influence on who we are and who we're becoming than the people around us.

Jim Rohn famously said, "You are the average of the five people you spend the most time with." I spend a lot of time with my kids. I'm assuming this explains why my wife tells me that I act like a child sometimes. Regardless, the point Rohn is making is that you are heavily influenced by those whom you allow to influence you, consciously or subconsciously.

Evaluating your circle of influence is a matter of identifying what needs are currently being met, where gaps may exist, and where you need to forge new relationships.

This is a concept I teach in my "Advancing Your Career" program. I speak about the role of an inner circle as it relates to one's personal and professional progression.

I invite you to complete the same exercise that I ask every participant to do.

Write the names of the top five people who have the most influence in your life. These can be friends, family members, colleagues, bosses. Then identify which needs that individual meets for you. Examples: love, support, encouragement, listener, friendship.

When I completed this exercise, my wife, Whitney, was and still is in my top five. She meets my needs of support, love, friendship, and a host of other needs as a friend and spouse. She's awesome.

A gap she doesn't fill for me, however, is one of an entrepreneur. Whitney is a teacher, and that's pretty close to being the antithesis of an entrepreneur. There's a lot of stability in teaching, especially as it relates to income. I can speak to Whitney about my business and she's a great listener. She's supportive. She's encouraging. What she can't provide is an understanding of what keeps me awake at night. I can talk with her about new marketing ideas and, again, she'll provide an awesome ear for the conversation. She won't necessarily share her thoughts on whether my marketing idea is good or if it needs improvement.

Similarly, as I look at my inner circle of friends, I notice that none of them relate to what it was like to go into business for yourself. I love my friends, and each of them is tremendously successful in their own careers. But being an entrepreneur is different.

To dissect it further, I have some siblings who are successful entrepreneurs. I talk with them about business. Their insight is always appreciated. Yet even then, none of them owns a business quite like mine. How they market, sell, and deliver their services is different than what I have found to be effective in my line of work.

That's my gap.

Therefore I needed to be intentional in forging relationships with people who could relate to my experience in running a speaking and coaching business. With every new endeavor I take on, such as this book, one of my biggest priorities in ensuring success is to always build relationships with people who have already accomplished what I am setting out to do.

Sometimes our friendships naturally progress to mimic our current state of life. When you're young and single, you hang out with others who are young and single. When you start dating someone else, you probably still hang out with the single crowd, as long as your public displays of affection don't nauseate your freewheeling friends.

When you get married, you may hang out with your single friends for a bit, but the frequency may begin to decline. Before long, married couples begin to see less of their single friends. They hang out more with other married couples, if they go out at all. A new circle of friends emerges.

Then when a married couple branches off and has a child, they really slack off in going out... with *anyone*. They're freaking exhausted. They don't see their single friends, who usually have no idea how much energy is required to raise a kid. Eventually, you stop getting invited out entirely, which is usually fine by the married couple with a newborn anyway.

Married-with-kids couples then meet other married-with-kids couples. They interact at the playground or the day care center.

They realize they're experiencing similar things. They talk about the stage their kid is in and who is experiencing what. They talk about who puked on who and which baby had the absolute worst diaper blowout of the century.

If they like each other, they'll begin to have playdates together. I use the term "playdate" as an all-encompassing get-together. These playdates can include a time when the kids actually play together or a time when the moms just want to chat with another adult human. Sometimes it's when just the parents get together as an excuse to drink, without the guilt of being the only irresponsible parent on earth!

It's a natural, somewhat magnetic, progression. Singles hang with singles. Couples hang with couples. Marrieds hang with marrieds. Married with kids hang with married with kids. And finally, retirees move to Sun City to hang out with other retirees.

Attitude can be just as magnetic. Positive people typically enjoy spending time with other positive people. Similarly, and detrimentally, negative attitudes will gravitate toward more negativity. Tiggers will find other Tiggers, and Eeyores will find more Eeyores.

If you want to be a manager, forge relationships with people in management. If you want to be an entrepreneur, create friendships with entrepreneurs. If you want to be more positive, spend more time with positive people. If you're in a relationship with someone who doesn't help elevate you to become a better person, get out of the relationship. If you recognize you're surrounded by friends who are always whining and complaining about everything, make new friends.

Who holds you accountable to fulfill the bold declarations you make? Where you can expose your hurt, your dreams, and your fears in a non-judgmental environment? Who expresses empathy while never crossing the line of encouraging complacency? Who understands your frustration without allowing you to wallow in resignation?

Who better to push you to go beyond your comfort zone than someone else who is doing the same thing for themselves? How effective can someone be as a source of encouragement and positivity for you when their own insecurity and jealousy consume them? How can you hold yourself, and be held, to a higher standard when those around you are mired in mediocrity?

It is both possible and necessary to "outgrow" people sometimes. This isn't a matter of thinking we're better than someone else. It's recognizing that where you are now and where you want to go may be more than what someone else is willing to do with his or her own life. At some point, they'll no longer support your own personal growth and development. Not only will some people choose not to support you any further, they may become passive or active detriments to your personal success. You must move beyond these people.

There is much to learn from others who have achieved that which we hope to also achieve. But for some reason, people hold themselves back from forging such crucial relationships. They close their ears to another's insight. "They just don't understand," they say. Let me be clear about this: Your situation, while personal to you, is not unique. To believe that no one on earth could ever understand your precise situation is simply an excuse for not opening up to the possibility that perhaps you are meant for something greater than where you are today.

People before you have experienced similar things. They have gone through what you're going through. They have achieved what you hope to achieve. They have stumbled far more often than you have. You are not the first to be in a situation like this. You will not be the last, either.

All fears become compounded when we attempt to face them alone. We shy away from opening ourselves up to others because we're afraid of being judged. We fear how someone will look at us, or what they will think about us, if they knew how we really felt or what we really thought.

What we fail to recognize is that by admitting our fear, by calling it out for what it is, we minimize the strangling grip it has on us. To keep a fear bottled up causes it to grow into a larger fear. We need people in our lives who encourage us to call out our fears and get in front of them.

As a kid, did you ever have a fear that a monster lived in your closet? I did. I would lie in my bed and just know with certainty that something was in there, ready to chew me into pieces and end my brief life.

I was also convinced that someone was under my bed at night. I'm pretty sure watching one of the *Friday the 13th* movies as a young kid didn't help my paranoia.

The monster in my closet and the killer under my bed would mentally torture me. I contemplated opening the closet door to find out if the monster was there. I'd choose not to because I'd imagine that as soon as I opened the door, the monster would pull me in, close the door, and I'd never be seen or heard of again.

The psycho under my bed would pull me under the bed if I looked. I'm somewhat claustrophobic so the idea of struggling with a madman under my bed was enough to keep me awake.

Looking back, it's easy to say these are silly fears. There's no such thing as monsters and no one is waiting silently under my bed to kill me. What's interesting is that while my fears may have changed, the imagination of what could go wrong has not.

Notice that my hesitation to open the door or to look under the bed included two fears: One, what I believed to be there. Two, what would happen if my fears were true.

I feared the monster in the closet I could not see, and I feared the imagined possibility of what would happen if a monster were there.

Eventually, I outgrew those fears, but they have circled back with my own boys. When my oldest son, Finnegan, said something about a monster in the closet, my initial response was, "There's no such thing as monsters." I'm pretty sure my parents said the same thing to me as a boy, and I certainly understand that as an adult. It didn't alleviate my fear as a kid and I wasn't surprised when it didn't alleviate his fear, either.

The next time he mentioned a monster, I decided to play the hero. I went over and opened up the closet doors, ready to pounce on whatever monster might be lurking. Of course, nothing was in there, which satisfied him momentarily. As long as I was there, he felt safe.

The most recent time I heard about the monster, I took an entirely different approach. When Finn said, "There's a monster in my closet," instead of dismissing his irrational fear, instead of trying to save the day for him, I encouraged him to invite the monster to join us.

The look on Finn's face was one of absolute bewilderment. Invite it out to eat us? Have you lost your mind? He started laughing because the idea of that was so absurd to him.

I encouraged him again. "Let's call to him. Let's invite him out," I said.

"Hello in there," we called. "Come on out." Nothing. No movement.

"Maybe he's being shy," I said. "Go open the door for him. Maybe he'll come out then."

Again, Finn had a look of absolute horror. Not only was I suggesting that we invite the monster out to invariably eat us, now I was suggesting we open the door for it.

I encouraged him again. "Go ahead. Open the door. Let's see if he'll join us."

Reluctant but willing, Finn got out of his bed and opened the closet door to invite the monster out.

"He's not here," Finn said.

"Too bad," I said. "I think it would have been fun to hang out with him. We could have asked him what it's like to live in a silly closet."

Finn laughed. "Maybe we can invite him out if he comes back again," he said.

"Of course we can. He's probably a really nice monster. I bet he'd love to laugh with us."

Finn hopped back in bed, more confident that the monster was no longer looming in the closet. I haven't heard him mention anything about the monster since. If he does, I'll encourage him to invite him out all over again.

I share this story for a number of reasons. First, in the interest of full disclosure, the idea to invite the monster out was not mine. I learned this approach from another parent who shared their similar experience with me. I think this speaks to the importance of surrounding yourself with people who can help elevate you to where you want to be.

Second, this exposed a fear of mine, which is that I may not always be there to protect my kids. If you're a parent, you may share a similar desire to shield your children from harm, to be the mighty protector they believe you to be. It even feels great to be their hero, and the idea that I might not always be that for them scares me.

Third, this approach does something greater for them than having me be my child's protector. This taught Finn the importance of addressing his fears directly. At some point in my children's lives, I won't be able to help them address every fear they have. My job as a parent is not to be the one to solve all of their problems, but to help them become someone who is capable of solving their own problems.

Finally, by calling out the fear and addressing it face to face, it minimized the scariness around the fear. It shrunk the fear factor. It released the grip. It made the situation manageable.

At this point in their lives, my kids need my help in learning how to confront their fears. Today their fears are of things that don't exist: monsters in the closet, Swiper the Fox, and other fears that stem from wild imaginations.

Their future fears will be undoubtedly different but they'll possess the possibility of being just as paralyzing. Presently, I am that person in their life who can help them get beyond their fears.

I wonder, who do you have in your life who is helping you do the same today?

WHO ARE YOU TO OTHERS?

Up until now, I've asked you to consider who your circle of influence is. Now I want you to think about who you are to others who include you in their circles.

Do you find that your friends seek you out to share their drama filled fiasco of a life? People like that possess the ability to make your ears bleed with stories of how other people have done them wrong. They insist on telling you the latest tale of their misfortune and how no one's life could possibly suck any worse than theirs.

These people are Eeyores. They are the woe-is-me people roaming the earth, sucking the life out of everything in their path. They are the whiners, the complainers, the downers. They are the ones who leave you feeling physically, emotionally, mentally, and spiritually drained by the end of the conversation. They may not be the initial reason why alcohol was created but they definitely provide a reason to drink it.

They are also consistent, persistent, and opportunistic. They consistently view things through a lens of negativity and pessimism. They are persistent in their pursuit to make you the same way. They seek the opportunity to lure someone of weak mind to join their ranks.

If you are constantly being approached by Eeyores, take a look in the mirror. You may think you're being kind by lending a sympathetic ear or providing a shoulder to cry on, but you might also be encouraging this insidious behavior. Perhaps listening to their woes makes you feel better about yourself. Maybe they give you some great material for conversations with other people. Maybe they're filling your need to be needed.

Regardless of why Eeyores are in your life, run away from them as fast as you possibly can. People of significance don't have drama in their lives because they refuse to allow drama to stay in their lives. I consider myself a good listener, but not for Eeyores. I do not make myself available to swim in the pool of misery with them. I have better things to think about. I have more meaningful things to accomplish. So do you.

What value do you bring to your circle? Be the person in your circle who encourages others to achieve more, to push beyond their comfort zones. Don't get caught up providing sympathy when you could exhibit more empathy instead. Say the tough thing and encourage your friend or colleague to take charge of their own life. Be the person that makes a positive difference in the life of someone else.

Marianne Williamson[3] talks about our fear in a very simple, powerful message that I think sums it up: "Our deepest fear is not that we are inadequate. Our deepest fear is that we are powerful beyond measure. It is our light, not our darkness that most frightens us. We ask ourselves, 'Who am I to be brilliant, gorgeous, talented, fabulous?' Actually, who are you not to be?"

6

LETTING IT GO

"So much more can happen with our hands open. In fact, closing and stubbornly maintaining our grip is often what keeps us stuck, though we want to blame everything and everyone else, especially what we're holding on to."

~ Mark Nepo

once read a story by Mark Nepo in his book *The Book of Awakening: Having the Life You Want by Being Present to the Life You Have.*[4] It's a story that illustrates the importance of letting go. Here's an excerpt of the story:

> There is an ancient story from China that makes all this very clear. It stems from the way traps were set for monkeys. A coconut was hollowed out through an opening that was cut to the size of a monkey's open hand. Rice was then placed in the

carved-out fruit, which was left in the path of the monkeys. Sooner or later, a hungry monkey would smell the rice and reach its hand in. But once fisting the rice, its hand could no longer fit back out through the opening. The monkeys that were caught were those who would not let go of the rice.

As long as the monkey maintained its grip on the rice, it was a prisoner of its own making. The trap worked because the monkey's hunger was the master of its reach. The lesson for us is profound. We need to always ask ourselves, What is our rice and what is keeping us from opening our grip and letting it go?

Here's what I'm wondering: What's your rice? What are you still holding onto so tightly that it is preventing you from moving forward? What story are you continuing to tell that keeps you stuck in the past?

Notice that Nepo's story doesn't talk about the monkeys who got free. It makes no mention of the monkeys who grabbed a fistful of rice, recognized how they were stuck, and chose to let go of the rice.

The story focuses on the one who got caught. It focuses on the one who refused to release what no longer served them. Maybe they held on out of fear that this was their only opportunity for food. Maybe they kept their grip out of their own stubbornness, failing to admit that this particular venture wasn't going to work for them.

I wonder if the other monkeys tried to convince the trapped monkey to drop the rice. Perhaps they begged and pleaded (in whatever ways monkeys do that), to no avail. Perhaps there was one who shook her head and said, "I told you this was a bad idea." Maybe the trapped monkey dug in his dirty monkey heels to prove her wrong.

Maybe the one who got caught was just obeying a command or request given to him by another monkey. He could then hold onto the rice, get caught, and be irate because he was simply following orders. Not surprisingly, according to his tale, that other monkey conveniently fled the scene of the crime.

Maybe he grabbed the rice, recognized he was stuck and was convinced that, yet again, he always makes stupid decisions. This was more proof of that. Maybe he realized he wasn't going to amount to anything anyway. He might as well just wallow in self-defeat until someone else came along who could dictate the fate of his life.

Perhaps the caught monkey will reflect on his life, wishing he stuck to eating the lice that he used to pick off the love of his monkey life. Maybe he decided to hold onto the rice because he was so sick of eating lice. I don't know.

I'm pretty sure I've gotten the most I can from this monkey analogy. There are times we get stuck. But there is a big difference between *getting* stuck and *staying* stuck. Everyone gets stuck once in a while. Staying stuck is often due to our own behavior in that situation. We're the ones who hold ourselves back. We are our own rice.

It's often easy to recognize in others the things that hold them back. We witness someone staying in an abusive relationship. A woman is treated like crap by her boyfriend, yet she continues to make excuses for him, hoping in vain he'll change someday.

A manager wonders why he is constantly being passed over for a promotion without ever realizing that his own arrogance and sense of entitlement is what drives people from him.

Relationships become strained because one person is absolutely convinced that they were right about a situation. They're willing to completely break ties with another individual who, for some unbeknownst reason that they can't possibly fathom, doesn't see how right they are.

Easy for an outsider to see. Too often, those who are involved don't see with the same clarity.

Take Joe, for example. I met Joe in Phoenix, where I was to speak at a conference.

When we were on our way to the hotel, I asked Joe how his day was going.

"Just livin' the dream," he said, somewhat sarcastically.

Here we go, I thought.

"Is that right?" I asked. "How long have you been driving for Uber?"

"About a year," he said.

"You enjoy it?"

"It pays the bills," he said.

Is that what "living the dream" means, I wondered? How sad.

"How long have you lived in Phoenix?" I asked.

"I moved back here fifteen years ago. I used to live in San Francisco and also in Florida."

"That's a lot of travel," I said.

"When I was in ninth grade, my mom dragged me out here from San Francisco. I went to high school here and then went to Arizona State University."

"Oh, cool. How did you like ASU?"

"It was all right. I wasn't like an athlete or anything. And I wasn't into the Greek scene, either. The idea of paying for friends is, like, absurd to me. So I kind of kept to myself. The college also canceled my major a few times while I was there, so that was frustrating."

"What was your major?"

"Golf course management. They offered it, then didn't offer it, then offered it again. It was annoying. So I ended up with like two hundred college credits and I still don't have a degree."

"You plan on finishing up?" I asked.

"Nah. Lost interest. I was mainly interested in that degree because I golfed myself, before I got hurt."

"Sorry to hear that."

"Yeah. It sucks. I was playing in one of the US Open Qualifier tournaments when I hurt my back. Turns out I damaged two of my discs. That was the end of that. It kills me because I see some of these younger guys getting ready to go on the circuit and I trained them when they were younger.

"People talk about golf now and I don't want to hear it. I'm not into it anymore. I mean, I'll watch it occasionally but not often.

"And people lie about their golf game, you know? They talk about how they're a scratch golfer and I'm like 'No, you're not.' People cheat. They don't count all the strokes. I guess that's all right."

I sat silently. Joe seemed to be lost in his own web of thoughts.

He continued. "Sometimes I play at Top Golf with friends or co-workers. I can take a wedge and, like, bury the shots. They're always telling me 'Man, you should play professionally,' and I'm like, 'Yeah, I know but I can't because I hurt my back.' I'm just bitter, I guess."

Ya think? With every word, I was becoming more depressed. I couldn't wait to distance myself from such negativity. I'm not saying his situation isn't unfortunate, but continuing to be victimized by his past doesn't help him advance or move forward. That, in my opinion, is what's most sad.

Did Joe need a hug? Hell no. A swift kick would do him some good. Joe's a grown man. During a fifteen-minute car ride, to a total stranger he rattled off all the things that sucked about his life.

Joe's negativity was suffocating. It was clear he felt entitled to be further along in his life than where he was. Unfortunately, he'll stay stuck at his current level as long as his desire to be right about his situation remains of the upmost importance. There's nothing significant about this current track.

In his mind, Joe is a victim. He has been victimized by his mom, his college, his body, and a slew of other things we never had the pleasure to discuss. Instead of positively and proactively discussing ways to improve his situation, Joe spends his time trying to justify what he deemed to be an inadequate life by showcasing how he's been dealt such a difficult hand. Grow up, Joe.

Harsh synopsis on my part? Possibly, but I emphatically call attention to this type of mindset because of the devastating consequences it produces: the consequence of accepting the most unfortunate aspects of life as your hopeless new norm.

Joe's story is not unique. Plenty of people continue to tell their tales of what could have been if only there were a different set of circumstances. They succumb to the belief that they are powerless to change their misfortune into something positive. Instead, they lower their self-expectations with the hope that others will expect less of them as well.

The plight of the victim is not that something bad has happened to them. It's not that they have, in some cases, been victimized. It's that in their minds they became a victim, which became their identity. There is a stark difference between stating "I have been victimized" and "I am a victim." Nouns are so much more difficult to change than verbs.

LIMITING EMOTIONAL NEEDS

Many people limit their success, their happiness, their fulfillment, and their significance because of their own perceived emotional needs. Some have an incessant need to get in the last word of every conversation. You know that last word? That last little dig right at the end of a conversation. The last little zing, jab, twist of the knife that continues to drip fuel onto a flame.

It's "Maybe next time you'll be a little smarter about it," or "That was stupid"—the end-of-conversation statements that turn smoldering embers into raging fires. When the need to be right and the need to get in the last word collectively join forces, you may hear something like, "I told you so" or "You should have listened to me in the first place."

One day I was sitting in Starbucks doing some work. A mother and daughter sat next to me and began talking to each other. For the most part, I paid them no attention.

During their conversation, both of them became increasingly agitated. They started talking slightly louder to each other. I do not know about the daughter's specific activity the mother was referencing, but I knew mom didn't approve of it.

The conversation was concluding in this way:

Mom: "Make sure you never do that again."

Daughter: "I know, mom. I *said* I wouldn't."

Mom: "I know. I'm just saying that was really dangerous and you could have gotten hurt."

Daughter: "Mom, I get it. I *know*. I said I wouldn't do it again."

Mom: "Ok, it's just that I worry about you."

Daughter: "God, I *know* already. I said I wouldn't do it again."

I wondered at what point one of them would be content to simply stay silent. The point was made and understood. Anything said after that was simply to satisfy their individual desire to have the last word. The desire has shifted from addressing the issue to stroking the ego.

The need to be right is another example of a wedge driven into the fabric of conversations, relationships, and worldviews.

We have created a profession out of mediation, the process whereby a third party joins a conversation because the original two people can't get past their own pride and ego and see each other's point of view. This is the adult version of calling in mom and dad to settle an argument between the children. Are you kidding me?

The danger in being consumed by the need to be right is the minimizing benefits of achieving that goal. You can absolutely be right in almost every aspect of your life, and there's a good chance that you will absolutely suffer because of it.

Seeking validation that you are right is, in essence, a desire for others to deem you, your intellect, your integrity, your competence, or your judgment as worthy, correct, and above reproach. When people don't get that validation in a satisfactory way, they become frustrated, angry, hurt, and dejected. Resentment takes residency within their thoughts.

Resentment is also possible in those moments when we've been treated unfairly or wronged by some standards. Perhaps your achievements haven't been recognized in a way that highlighted your commitment, your sacrifice, or your resilience in the matter. Worse, maybe someone else who benefitted from your hard work is the one being glorified. Think about moments in your life when you have experienced this. Were there not deep and intense emotions about the incident?

Were these people wrong for not seeing all you've done for your friends, your family, your team, or your company? Were they wrong not to recognize how you were the one slighted in this case? Were they wrong not to understand how insulting their behavior toward you was?

Yes, they were wrong. Yes, you were right. And for winning, your prize is a heavy bag you'll carry everywhere you go. People stopped caring about how right you were a long time ago. They've moved on. Have you?

"You don't know me or my situation," you might be saying. It's true. I don't. But I don't need to. It makes no difference if I became adamant about how right you are. My opinion doesn't change what happened. I'm not here to discredit your position or to justify it. Nor am I trying to play the "my situation is worse than yours" game. I'm merely recognizing that the one who carries the resentment is the one who remains hurt the longest.

Anger, while devastating in its own right, is typically a burst of intense emotion that hurts everyone in its wake. It's a difficult emotion to keep at a heightened state, though. It's not uncommon to feel somewhat exhausted after an outburst. It's also when resentment kicks in, and resentment has the temperament to last a lifetime.

Resentment can be intoxicating in a way in which a drunk starts to believe he's stronger than he is. The most comforting part about replaying the hurtful situation is that in our memory we are always right. Resentment—like the rice in the coconut— has the ability to keep us trapped in the past, jaded in the present, and cynical about the future.

Oddly enough, as damaging as it can be to hold onto, it's surprisingly simple to do so.

Why do people continue to replay their painful past, experiencing yet again the facts and the feelings associated with that event? It affects them physically, emotionally, and mentally. Even those who profess that they have moved on or those who claim they want to move on continue to play the same scenario repeatedly in their minds.

For some, they do this because they believe it keeps them from getting hurt in the same way a second time. If they were taken advantage of previously, they become hellbent on never letting that happen again.

For others, replaying their perceived offenses (and in no way am I saying they aren't legitimate offenses) influences their belief that somehow the justice they are due for their hardship will become recognized. In their minds, if they let it go, who else will remember it when the time for acknowledgment and retribution comes back around? Unfortunately, resentment provides only the illusion of ever getting satisfactory restitution they feel they deserve.

What becomes infuriating to the one holding onto the resentment is that, while they are the one experiencing a very personal and powerful emotion, it seems to have no ill effect on the person to which it is directed. The victim is taking meds to soothe their anxiety and depression while the offender is sipping a Mai Tai on the beach in Cancun.

Not only does the past incident enrage them but the perception that it has no lasting effect on the person who initiated such an offense is equally as appalling. The harbored pain has far exceeded the ability to be of some use to any individual. Stress, heath issues, sleeping difficulty, and dysfunctional relationships are potential results of harbored resentment and anger. When it's at its worst, it no longer gets addressed. It becomes the new norm.

Regarding the present and future, those who harbor resentment become prone to interpreting each new perceived act of unfairness as just more of the same. They are hyper vigilant, always looking at their life situations through a lens of "I won't be the victim again."

No offense is too trivial, lest they be caught unprepared. Thus, a heavy anchor and long chain begins to form. Each new incident of perceived injustice is nothing more than a new link to add to the chain.

Preparing for the worst easily shifts into *expecting* the worst. Someone who was once victimized can become a perennial victim, going through life with an altered perception of reality no matter the situation. Holding onto that anger and resentment won't change the past. It will only change how they see the present and future, which is far from a healthy and balanced perspective.

You may think that resentment and anger only influence one's personal life and that it doesn't translate into someone's profession. Nothing could be further from the truth. Remember that the line between our personal and professional lives is an illusion. One aspect of our life will always influence the other in some way.

Here's an example. Jack resents his boss because he believes that he is never appreciated for his contributions. When he's passed over for a promotion, his belief becomes more justified.

Jack hasn't been sleeping well since the promotion was offered to someone else. Because he's not sleeping, he's not feeling refreshed in the morning. He's been short with his wife and recently started to get testy with his kids. Not only did he harbor the resentment for his boss, he was now developing feelings of guilt regarding his treatment of his family.

Lately, he's been driving to work annoyed. He's not excited. He's not engaged. He's pissed, and the traffic he encounters during his commute only irritates him more.

Upon his arrival one morning, he is accosted by an employee who has an urgent problem to solve. Jack wonders why he's the only one who can think of solutions. Clearly, always being the one with the answers hasn't caught the attention of his superiors, *so screw them*. Let the team figure out their own answers. When they begin to struggle, upper management will finally recognize that Jack has always been the brains of the operation.

His behavior toward his employee begins to strain. He is increasingly irritated with everything and everyone, and he's struggling to control his temper. He lashes out at his employees one too many times, and human resources gets involved.

When asked about the situation, Jack mentions how what he said was taken out of context. It's just a misunderstanding.

Human resources registers Jack for a training session on becoming a more effective communicator. If communication is the issue, certainly training should help.

Reluctantly, Jack attends the training a couple of weeks after the incident. He resents that he's even there. *Don't they know how good of a communicator I am?*

The trainer starts the class and Jack's worst nightmare comes true. Some all-too-smiley trainer begins to share surface-level tips on how to be a better communicator. Internally, Jack is stewing. He thinks of all the people at his work who should be sitting in this training. After all, they're the ones who need it.

He is consumed by thoughts of the amount of work that's piling up on his desk while he attends this useless training. He checks his watch, three times every hour, until finally the training concludes.

When he gets back home, his lovely wife asks, "How was your day?"

"I had to attend that bullshit training on communication today," Jack spits. "Total waste of time."

His wife smiles, secretly wondering how she can bash in his head with the mirror that she wishes he'd finally look into.

Jack's problem may or may not be with his communication, but it definitely involves his choosing to not let go of his resentment. In his mind, he was right and his boss was wrong, and he's choosing to carry that with him every day.

Imagine if what you thought to be true for twenty-five years of your life turned out to be false. How would you feel upon learning that you had been manipulated and lied to by the ones you loved and trusted the most?

Not only that, what if the lies you were told greatly affected and possibly ruined the life you could have had with someone else that you loved? If ever there were an opportunity to resent someone, this would certainly be it.

Such was the case for Ryan Thomas, the creator of Ryan Thomas Speaks.

Raised by his divorced mom, Ryan was brought up believing that his dad didn't love him, didn't care about him, and only caused chaos in his life. He was told that the only ones who truly loved him were his mom and her extended family, which Ryan referred to as "The Regime." He was alienated from his dad for almost three decades of his life because of these deeply engrained beliefs. Finally, Ryan succumbed to the stress and pressure and ultimately severed ties with his dad, a decision that was instigated and celebrated by his mom.

After a decade of no contact with his dad, Ryan began to suspect that much of what he had been told about his dad wasn't exactly true. As he matured and started his adult life, the stories he had been told started to fall apart. He recognized that what his mom was categorizing as "love" was actually her own selfishness, hatred, and need to control the situation.

Ryan secretly started to reconnect with his dad. What he came to learn was that his dad was nothing like the man he was made out to be. He was kind. He loved Ryan tremendously. He always wanted a relationship with Ryan but was denied access for years.

Once reconnected with his dad, Ryan had plenty of reason to turn his anger, frustration, and resentment toward his mother and extended family who had deprived him of this relationship for so long.

Instead, Ryan used his experience to benefit the lives of others in similar situations. He created Ryan Thomas Speaks, and now helps alienated parents reconnect with their children in much the same way he did with his own father.

He has written books about parental alienation. He's created programs for alienated parents to learn more about how they can reconnect with their kids. Ryan works with parents in over twenty-five countries and is asked to speak on this topic throughout the world. Now, Ryan is widely considered an expert in his field, primarily because he had the courage to expose this terrible phenomenon through the eyes of a child who experienced it firsthand.

Not to be forgotten, however, is the forgiveness he extended to his mom. If he grew up loving his mom and hating his dad, then switched to loving his dad but hating his mom, the experience would be nothing more than a transfer of hatred. He would have stayed stuck.

What's remarkable about Ryan's experience is that he has now developed strong relationships with both parents. He took a tremendously difficult situation and created something meaningful around it.

Significance.

CLARITY AND A DEADLINE

I think we should allow ourselves to feel the full range of emotions that arise in given situations. Even the most zen-like among us are vulnerable to experiencing the extreme highs and lows that life throws at us.

To be fully yourself, to experience true freedom, you must get comfortable expressing your emotions in a productive way. Yes, it takes internal courage and strength to expose ourselves to another in such a vulnerable way. Doing so releases much of the tension, stress, and ill will that gets harbored deep within us. Like the ability to maintain our resentment, releasing it can be equally as intoxicating.

To communicate our feelings effectively requires that we spend time digging to find the root cause of them. If you're pissed off at someone, it's not enough to turn into the huge green monster and destroy everything that you see. When you force yourself to trace back the source of your emotion, you'll recognize that, more often than not, you're making the situation mean something about you.

When I tell my kids to get ready for bed seventeen times in one hour, my blood pressure begins to rise. It's easy for me to raise my voice to a decibel that makes the windows rattle. Sadly, I've done this more than once.

Most of time, I get the response I want, which is the immediate compliance of my boys. Long term, I feel like a worthless ass. The guilt sets in and I consider nominating myself for the World's Worst Father award.

When I think about the deeper source and explore what I make that situation mean about me, I realize it has more to do with my frustration that I haven't been consistent with our bedtime routine. I'm too controlling, even though I explicitly stated earlier in this book that we only control our choices, not people.

The source can be a fear of not being respected, compounded with the slightly unrealistic expectation that if I say something once I shouldn't have to say it again. I'm sure there are other factors as well.

What do all of these sources of my anger and frustration have in common? Me. My thoughts. My issues. My judgments. This situation has more to do with me than it does them.

As I write this, being transparent and real with you isn't easy. Likewise, your own self-reflection may be difficult for you at first. What it provides, however, is a little clarity around the emotion, which then gives the opportunity for productive next steps.

Too often, people haven't learned how to handle these situations in a proactive, effective manner. They bottle up their emotions, possibly out of pride, or embarrassment, or fear of judgment. Feelings become mismanaged. People rely on eating or drinking away their self-displeasure. They seek an escape through medication of either the legal or illegal kind.

At its worst, some people harbor their anger for too long. In one fatal action, they take innocent lives in their attempts to right the perceived wrong. These are the most cowardly individuals of all.

Feel the array of emotions. Reflect on the source. Then give yourself a deadline of when you will choose to let it all go.

I was once invited to speak at a meeting with business owners and leaders in attendance. This engagement took place within the first year I ventured out on my own. This was a big opportunity for me. Done well, this could open doors into companies that otherwise didn't know I existed.

I prepared my content. I practiced my delivery. I eagerly awaited this opportunity.

It was an absolute disaster.

I was terrible. I don't mean that in some self-loathing, pity party kind of way. I mean it as much of a matter-of-fact kind of way I can relate. I just sucked.

I made a typical mistake of someone young who addresses that level of business executive. I had too much content to cram into a short amount of time. I lectured to them instead of providing concepts and encouraging group conversation. I tried to impress them with the extent of my knowledge. The result, and the feedback received afterwards, made me recognize they were anything but impressed.

When I returned home from that event, I was ready to shut the whole business down. I was furious with myself. Embarrassed. At one point I even blamed the executives for not recognizing all the good material I just provided for them. I was a mental mess. I didn't want to send another email out. I didn't want to talk to another prospective client. I wanted to sit in my misery.

For the rest of the day I did exactly that. I threw my very own pity party, at which I was the special guest.

During my mental temper tantrum, I allowed myself to feel the range of emotions at their deepest level. I held nothing back. I felt everything as hard as I could. I didn't try to spin it positively that I just wasn't very good that day; I allowed, even encouraged, myself to think that I was absolutely pathetic in that meeting because that's how I felt.

I allowed myself eight hours, from 2:00 p.m. until 10:00 p.m., to hate everything about what happened that day. I didn't try to put up a guard. I went mentally raw. I sucked, and I made sure I knew it, felt it, and expressed it within the timeframe that I provided.

Happily, long before 10:00 p.m. my mood, my feelings, and my thoughts began to shift. The speaking engagement almost became comical to me. I could shake my head in disbelief, but no longer felt weighted down by the intense negative emotions that had consumed me just a few hours prior.

For me, putting a framework around my emotions creates a space for freely feeling every emotion with the understanding that I will also let it go when it no longer serves me. If you're upset at something, get clear around the real reason why you're upset. Be upset. Feel upset. Express being upset, constructively. Then put a timeframe on it.

When will you move on from being upset? How long do you want give yourself to flush out the emotion and get yourself in a better frame moving forward? Eternity is not a legitimate option for a timeframe. It's hard to lead a life of significance if you're forever blinded by anger.

FORGIVENESS

There is no greater example of letting things go than extending your forgiveness to another. It may also be one of the most difficult decisions and actions to execute.

I often thought that those who teach about forgiveness must live glorious lives. Perhaps that was because I was too content to be right about my situations and didn't want to let them go. Maybe it's that I thought whoever talked about forgiveness certainly didn't understand my specific situation. In that sense, it was one of those ideas that could be really useful for someone else, but not me.

I used to feel that forgiveness was somehow excusing what someone else did previously. It almost felt wrong to forgive, as if that was somehow condoning the activity. That it justified it to an extent. Nothing could be further from the truth. If a dog bites me, I am free to forgive the dog. It doesn't mean I am forced to pet it again.

You might think forgiveness is only talked about in religious circles. For some, that would be grounds to dismiss it entirely. Yet the benefits I list below do not come from the Bible, the Quran, the Torah, or any other religious ideology. They come directly from the website of a well-respected medical organization, The Mayo Clinic.[5]

The benefits of forgiveness include: Healthier relationships. Greater spiritual and psychological well-being. Less anxiety, stress and hostility. Lower blood pressure. Fewer symptoms of depression. Stronger immune system. Improved heart health. Higher self-esteem.

There is something freeing about forgiveness, and the above list of benefits validates that feeling. As I view it now, I see it as a way to not let our past continue to define our present. No longer are we bound to live our present life in a hampered way by our past experiences. Forgiveness is yet another choice we get to make that influences the positive direction of our lives.

I could get all biblical on you and talk about the moral virtues of forgiveness. I'm not. I do believe in the validity of forgiveness.

I believe in the spiritual, physical, medical benefits of it, for certain. But I also don't think it's my place to mandate that one forgives another. Forgiveness is a personal choice, one I do hope you'll consider.

Sometimes, the hardest person to forgive is our own selves. But also the most critical if we are to ever move forward.

LETTING GO

Living a life of significance has as much to do with *taking on* as it does with *letting go*.

Declare today that you will let go of the belief that it is okay to live in mediocrity.

Let go of the need to always seek the approval of others. Seek council. Seek guidance. Do not live each day under the weighted fog of someone else's judgment about the direction of your life. Rise above your critics.

Let go of your perfectionist mindset. A person often claims to be a perfectionist as if it were a badge of honor. It's no such thing. It's a paralyzing, minimizing, dysfunctional way of being. Even perfectionists admit that there's no such thing as being perfect. Is it any wonder why they drive themselves and those around them crazy? They are admitting that what they're striving for is unattainable. To me, that sounds ridiculous.

Be attentive to detail. Be thorough. Use some forethought. Strive to be better today than you were yesterday.

But, please, spare me the perfectionist rhetoric.

Let go of the need to have more of the things that only bring superficial joy to your life. Refuse to be a shell of a human being whose sole goal is to fill his life with things that have no redeeming qualities. I feel sorry for those who live with an unquenched thirst for more, never fully basking in gratitude and fulfillment for what they have. Perhaps they are the ones who are to be pitied most of all.

Finally, let go of being the one person who holds you back from living a life that matters. Stop the charade. Take off the mask. Let the world see what you are capable of becoming. Be significant.

7

EMBRACE THE CRAZY

"If you lack the courage to make the plunge, all right! Stay where you are. But blame yourself, then; don't blame the job. And remember that 'desire' is not 'determination.' They begin with the same letter - but they don't end up on the same pinnacle of success."

~ James Cash Penney

You are created for something more.

Career advisors frequently ask their clients what they would do if they knew they couldn't fail. The thought is that the answer to this question reveals the direction one should take regarding their career endeavor.

I'm not a fan of this question. It assumes that failure is the worst possible outcome that anyone could ever encounter. You're better off asking someone what they would do if they knew they couldn't contract leprosy.

I think most successful people would say that their road to success was riddled with failure. They traveled the road not because they wouldn't fail, but because what they were pursuing was worth the occasional failure. The absence of failure was never the goal or the expectation. To proactively pursue something in life because you knew you couldn't fail is just not pursuing anything worthwhile.

Ask an Olympic athlete if she would still pursue a gold medal if she were guaranteed to win it. According to the mantra that we should wholeheartedly pursue those endeavors that presented no opportunity for failure, the athlete should leap with joy. However, I promise you, the opposite is true.

Her desire to train, to compete, and to celebrate would actually decrease if she knew there was absolutely no way she could fail. To those athletes, fulfillment comes from the hard work put in toward the achievement of that goal. It's about having the opportunity to compete against others who have committed themselves to a similarly worthy cause.

The most inspiring Olympic stories come from athletes who experienced struggle and hardships in their lives, yet learned how to be resilient and persevere. These stories reveal the sacrifices that were made by themselves and of those who supported them. If they're fortunate enough to be a medal winner, they stand on the podium with tears streaming down their face, not because of the medal in their hands but because of what earning that medal required of them.

To them, it's as much about the process as it is the result.

Just as an Olympic athlete's motivation would decrease if the gold medal were guaranteed, so too does our motivation to pursue our dreams if failure isn't an option. This is exactly what legendary football coach Vince Lombardi was referring to when he said, "I firmly believe that any man's finest hour, the greatest fulfillment of all that he holds dear, is that moment when he has worked his heart out in a good cause and lies exhausted on the field of battle—victorious."

Lombardi spoke of the discipline, the struggle, and the battle that one endures when attempting to achieve something that matters. I care very little about what you would do if you knew you could not fail because that tells me nothing about the strength of your commitment. I do not get excited about the first place winner who willfully competes against inferior opponents. I care very much, however, about what you're willing to commit to knowing in advance that you may encounter failure along the way.

If you do not experience failure, you will never grow into what you are fully capable of becoming. If you never encounter an obstacle in your path, you will never expand your aptitude, attitude, fortitude, or gratitude for the journey you are on. The mind and body respond to the proper stressors, almost yearning to be pushed beyond what is comfortable. To avoid the obstacle is to deprive the mind.

Neither failure nor the obstacles you encounter are ever the iron gates at the dead end you make them out to be. That dubious honor rests within you alone. Your mindset makes them such. For the small-minded, they provide firm evidence as to why retreat is the only option. For the significant-minded, they are yet another challenge and opportunity to forge ahead.

THE WIDEST GAP IN THE UNIVERSE

There is an internal struggle within the hearts of man. One desire is to be accepted, to live in comfort, to stay safe, to protect oneself by any measure. The other desire is the longing to stand out, to be and make a difference, and push oneself beyond the boundaries of complacency.

Therein lies the conflict, most evident for all to see in the widest gap of the universe: the gap between what you *say* and what you *do*.

Consider for a moment that if something were that important to you, you would have already figured out a way to get it done. If it truly mattered to you, you'd already have found an answer for it. If you haven't found the answer for it yet, maybe it's just not that important.

Many people confuse convenience with commitment. They describe what they "wish" or "want" in life but they don't do anything to achieve those things. They're likely to talk about how they think their life could be enhanced with the object of their desire but they don't admit that they're simply not willing to do what is necessary to obtain it.

What is it that you want? What is standing in your way? What do you need to *do*?

People tell me they wish they had more time to spend with their families, but they don't do anything to create more time with them.

Others tell me they want to be more financially comfortable but they don't do anything to change their earning, spending, or saving habits. Still others tell me they want to work in a better office environment, but they don't want to make the effort to create such an environment.

When people hear that I spent the entire month of July in Ireland with my family, they tell me how much they wish they could have that opportunity. One person went as far as to say, "I would give anything to be able to do that." If that were true, this person would already be making plans for an Ireland adventure. Of course, they're not. It seems ironic that someone would claim they'd give anything for something and yet do nothing for it.

When pressed for why these people haven't altered their behavior that could increase the odds of achieving what they want, their tap dance begins. Their energy and focus are no longer centered on what they proclaim to want. They now frantically search for an answer as to why they couldn't possibly achieve it. They search for an answer that will be most acceptable to the one with whom they are speaking.

The gap between saying and doing is like a treacherous mine field of excuses, blame, rationalization, justification, confusion, denial, and acquiescence. These, among others, are our self-protective weapons of choice. They keep our ego protected and our progress stagnant.

Thus, circumstances become the scapegoat for everything good that was never achieved.

YOUR WINNING STRATEGY

Consider why you haven't pursued that which you say you want. Actually, think about how you've explained to others why you haven't achieved that which you say you want. Therein lies your winning strategy.

Human beings want to win or, at minimum, we don't want to lose. When we perceive that we are unable to achieve something, we don't typically find it acceptable to admit our shortcomings. Instead, we need to create or find a reason why we fell short, a reason that is unquestioningly acceptable.

The beauty of the human mind is often found in its creativity. The way we maneuver between the gap of saying and doing is really a work of art. The ability to go through the list of self-protective weapons and choose the most appropriate one is fascinating to watch. Of course, it doesn't serve us in the least, other than providing a temporary redirection around the fact that we've chosen not to succeed.

What excuses have you used to justify why you're not moving forward? I assume time or money could be a top of that list. Those are nice, safe bets. They also seem to be the most common culprits of crushing personal dreams. It's like riding the merry-go-round in the land of the lost. We just never seem to have enough of either one.

Who would you like to blame for your current state of stagnation? Your boss? Your family? The guy at the DMV who gave you a funny look?

It was easy to blame the government, the banks, and the mortgage providers for the housing crisis a number of years ago. Certainly they played a role in that crash. I wonder, however, when we will point the finger back at ourselves.

Did we collectively forget simple math and economics? Did we ignore the fact that being *approved* for the million-dollar home does not mean we should *buy* the million-dollar home? Did we not think that we would need a certain income to pay the monthly mortgage payment? Is it someone else's fault that we left our calculator home the day that common sense begged us to pay it some attention?

We can always blame politicians for the laws, regulations, and corruption that plagues our country. Our political system is riddled with blame. Each party points to the other as being the reason why something bad happened. For many citizens, witnessing this type of behavior triggers our anger. It cries out for accountability and ownership. Yet we bring the exact same tactic into our personal and professional lives.

Entitlement exists within this mentality. If we feel slighted, we rage against the person, the system, even our luck as the cause of our unfortunate lot. Athletes who don't make the team blame the coach. Teams that don't win blame the referees. Parents with struggling children blame the schools. Schools with struggling students blame the system and the parents.

It's all just a game to determine who can hold the weight of responsibility for why someone's life isn't where they want it to be. They are owed success, and the absence of it surely can't be of their own volition.

So please, tell me. Who or what do you want to blame for your refusal to rise above, to take ownership, to get a grip on yourself, and to move forward?

Perhaps you've chosen to stay in a state of confusion. You choose to know just enough to not be viewed as clueless but you never get clarity on exactly what's happening around you. This is very strategic on your part. Where there is ambiguity, there is no accountability. If you knew exactly what the problem was, you might be responsible for fixing it. But if you don't understand the problem, how could ever possibly be expected to help solve it? Good for you. You've successfully avoided responsibility again.

RATIONALIZATION

My favorite, and the one that happens to be my personal self-protective weapon of choice, is rationalization. I have been gifted with the ability to make things make sense. This is a blessing and a curse, depending on how I use it.

To me, rationalization is so much more powerful than making excuses or placing blame. At this stage in my life, I feel uncomfortable making excuses about something. It's like how you feel when you vomit in your mouth. Placing blame on someone else has a similar effect. Please don't misunderstand me. Because I do not prefer to make excuses or to place blame on others in no way makes me better than anyone else. Quite the contrary. I might be the worst of all.

In the movie *The Usual Suspects*, the character "Verbal" Kint, played by Kevin Spacey, said, "The greatest trick the devil ever pulled was convincing the world he didn't exist." In many ways, that's exactly the danger posed by a gifted rationalizer. They subtly make it seem that whatever the outcome was, it's exactly as it should have been.

It's so difficult to argue the logic of the rationalizer. The student can say, "I didn't perform well on one exam because I spent my time studying for another." Makes sense to me.

The citizen says, "I don't have to pay taxes because the government just wastes our money anyway. Besides, the tax money I *didn't* pay was donated to a charity that does great work." A tax evader and a philanthropist rolled into one.

A father can't be expected to attend his child's soccer game because his boss imposed a stiff deadline that needs to be adhered to. Meeting this deadline and keeping his job provides the opportunity for his son to play soccer. Makes sense.

A single woman explains that she's not currently dating because she wants to focus on her career. She wants to get ahead first so that she's in a better position when she does meet the right person. Never mind that maybe she's still feeling the grief of a relationship gone sour or that she consistently seems to date classless men who don't treat her well.

Married couples get divorced because, hey, they simply grew apart. They try to convince themselves and others that the kids are handling the divorce really well, too, so much better than the parents would have imagined. It must be because even the kids recognize that their parents are better off separately than together. Rationalize.

A professional stays working in a job he can't stand because he has a family to support. His misery is his cross to bear for his kids to enjoy every new toy marketed in commercials. He gets upset when he feels his efforts are not appreciated nearly as much as they should be. This is the battle cry of the martyr.

All of these examples seem reasonable, logical, and tough to argue against. Not only are they tough to discredit, they can also be viewed as the best course of action. Rationalizations are wrapped in elements of truth. And that's exactly why rationalization is so powerful and outright destructive.

Rationalization is not lying. A rationalization might even be a half truth. It's like the weight loss company advertising how their meals have one-third less calories without also mentioning that they're using one-third the portion size. Kind of believable, but kind of garbage, too.

Any anger you might feel by reading the above scenarios is nothing but your own guilt about the situation. Your anger toward me is nothing more than a reflection of the anger within yourself. I'm not here to make you wrong nor am I here to be right. I'm here to call out the reality of the situation, because unless you recognize it, you'll never get past the shallow and bogus reasons you keep spewing as to why you're current situation isn't what you had hoped it would be.

Your winning strategy isn't designed to help you achieve your goal. It's the way in which you avoid the true explanation for your shortcoming, which is far more damaging to the ego than anything else. If you can adequately convince, deflect, or relinquish responsibility for your own situation, such that no one, including yourself, could possibly expect anything different, you win.

Listen, if it is that important to you, you'll find a way to do it. Simple as that.

THE "B" WORD

If what makes rationalizations so dangerous is how easy they are to accept, than the most destructive rationalization of all is our love and use of the word "busy."

As a society, we have fallen in love with this word. We use it as a reason why we haven't connected with someone in a while. We use it as a way to describe how things are at work. We use it to justify why we've let some balls drop.

Busy is not always used in a negative sense. When things are going well, we say we're "busy, but *good* busy." Can we not think of a better word to use in this sense?

What makes "busy" so powerful? The fact that every person accepts it of you is because they use it themselves with others.

Let's be bold here. You're not as busy as you make yourself out to be. You're just not. Oh, I know you have a lot of responsibility at work. You're running around with your kids. Your email inbox is flooded with people awaiting a response from you. You're very important but you're not that busy.

A client of mine wanted to connect more frequently with her sister. She recognized that it was too easy for the two of them to let weeks go by without speaking. While discussing this with me, she proceeded to rationalize why she hadn't reached out to her sister. She offered reason after reason after reason, all culminating with her perception of being so busy.

When she first uttered that word, I had to get past my own biased view of her situation. My client is a single female in her mid twenties. No kids. I immediately wanted to roll my eyes and shake my head. To me, if you don't have kids, you don't know busy.

A comparison mindset isn't beneficial, though. A couple with no kids can be busy, but busy with different activities. The couple with two kids can roll their eyes at the complaining couple with one child. The family with four kids looks at the family with two kids and talks about how easy they used to have it. The family of eight looks at everyone else and politely chuckles, knowing full well that ignorance is sometimes comical. Small families look at the family of eight and simply dismiss them as mentally insane.

We looked at my client's use of social media. She had Facebook status updates periodically posted throughout the day. We talked about her after-work routine, which consisted of working out, dinner, and spending time with her boyfriend. Occasionally, she had co-ed softball games. Busy. Busy. Busy.

By the time we fleshed out her week, we identified over ten hours of available time she had to chat with her sister. Morning and afternoon commute times. Lunch time. Time spent watching some of her favorite TV episodes. Time spent traveling to her boyfriend's house. Time spent in the car driving to her softball games. We hadn't even reviewed the weekend.

Being busy has become a social badge of honor. The idea that we're not busy suddenly conjures up images of someone who is a slacker. If you're not busy, you lack initiative. If you're not busy, you're not living up to your potential. If you're not busy, you're lazy.

Alternatively, if you're really busy, you must be really important. We live chaotic lives because, to some extent, it makes us feel good about ourselves and we look good through the eyes of others.

Professionally, God forbid we're not busy. If we're not busy, or if we aren't at least telling people at work how busy we are, we might catch the attention of our envious co-workers. They'll begin to think we're not pulling our share. They might start talking about us to others on the team. Our manager might actually reward our efficiency and effectiveness with more work. Best we always appear busy to keep under the radar and look really important.

Socially, there's pressure to do it all. We must experience everything we possibly can or somehow we haven't lived abundantly. We tout our progress, especially with technology, as being something to be revered. We're led to believe that more is better. More is more, and in many cases, more progress provides the opportunity for more problems.

Think about something as simple as connecting with another human being. Our ancestors used to write letters. Then we advanced to the phone. These days, if we don't want to connect on the phone, we can send an email. If we want to see the other person on the other line, we can use Skype or FaceTime. If we don't want to engage in a full conversation, we can send a text. If we want to get creative with short messages, we can send a Snapchat. If we don't want to live our lives at all, we can watch others live theirs through Facebook Live.

So many ways in which we can connect, yet we've become more disconnected from each other. We blanket our absence of connection in one simple word: busy.

But you're actually not that busy. You may just be distracted. Your priorities are out of alignment. Your perspective needs adjusting. You're just not that busy. Or, if you are, you don't need to be.

The "busy" person will often describe their busy life in certain phrases that come up in conversation. They will often describe in an exasperated tone what they "need to" do or what they "have to" do. They need to work late. They have to plan their three-year-old's birthday party. They have to go to the gym because they need to lose weight.

The use of the words is indicative of someone who is operating off of someone else's agenda. They're reactive, disempowering words. The mere thought of living life in a "need to" or "have to" mode increases stress and anxiety.

You don't "need to" or "have to" do anything. I want to know what you "choose to" do with your life. I want to know what you "get to" do with your life. I want to know what you "will do" with your life.

Nobody cares how busy you are or how hard you have it. Remove "busy" from your vocabulary. Try it for a week. See the difference it makes in your life.

It's time to take back the reins of your present and future. It's time to get clear on what you want. It's time to commit yourself to something worthy. Something that will challenge you, drive you, excite you, and terrify you. It's time to feel, possibly for the very first time, what it means to fully be alive.

It's time to burn the ships.

WHAT'S YOUR SHIP?

You might be familiar with Alexander the Great and Hernando Cortes. Separated in time by nearly two thousand years, both men were successful warriors. Among their many enemies, they're well known for battling the Persians and the Aztec Empire, respectively.

According to legend, while preparing to fight the enemy, both men ordered the destruction of their own ships. From their perspective, burning the ships removed any possibility of their men retreating if the fighting became too intense.

Being grossly outnumbered by the Persians, Alexander feared that his men would retreat to secure additional resources. Knowing the Persian navy was far superior, he believed that his men and boats would be easily destroyed by them. Therefore, he removed that escape route and told his men that they could return home only on Persian ships, which they did.

Cortes, from what I understand, did not actually burn his ships but scuttled them. He deliberately ran most of them aground, virtually rendering them useless. Again, faced with no retreat alternative, Cortes's men fought valiantly and defeated the Aztec Empire.

The validity of both legendary stories is hard to decipher. While the accuracy of each story is debatable, the concept of each is valid.

When retreat is no longer an option, the commitment to move forward and win is enhanced.

The idea of burning the ships can be misunderstood as encouraging reckless behavior. But it isn't an invitation to act foolishly, selfishly, or blindly. It's recognition that, at times, the safety net that provides a sense of security can also become the crutch that prevents your victory.

Most ventures, when you really consider everything that could happen, aren't truly "all or nothing" scenarios, as much as they appear to be in the moment. Most endeavors are not life or death. I don't find it necessary or smart to intentionally create a life or death situation. I do think, however, that it is worth looking at the safety nets in your life that might be holding you back.

In the book *Good to Great* by Jim Collins,[6] there is a story about Darwin Smith, the CEO of Kimberly-Clark. Shortly after Smith became CEO, he and his management team recognized that the core business of Kimberly-Clark—coated paper—was doomed to mediocrity.

They concluded that throwing the company into the consumer paper goods industry, where they would compete against the likes of Proctor & Gamble and Scott Paper, would ultimately determine their fate. Kimberly-Clark would either rise to the occasion or perish.

Smith decided to sell the mills, even the one in Kimberly, Wisconsin. The market downgraded the company's value, and people called his decision stupid at the time. Twenty-five years later, Kimberly-Clark owned Scott Paper and beat P&G in six of the eight product categories they competed in. Perhaps it wasn't so stupid after all.

Still too dramatic and risky for you? Here's an example of burning a ship on a much smaller scale.

When I first decided to venture out on my own in September 2011, I didn't know what I was doing. Looking back, I now see I was the poster child for how *not* to start a business. Seriously. At that point in my life, I had grown discontented with my professional career. I desired something different. I resigned from my position with no clear direction in sight.

I decided to give myself ninety days to figure out how to run a business and get some traction with new clients. I was excited to be out on my own. Terrified, for sure, but exhilarated, as well. Here's the problem: I didn't have a clue how to make it work.

The "build it and they will come" business plan doesn't actually work in reality, especially since I was still struggling to determine exactly what "it" was. My excitement turned to an agitated stress. I didn't know what I was doing. Worst of all, I didn't know what to do first.

It's an odd experience to go from spending most of your professional career interacting with large groups of coworkers to walking downstairs to a home office and interacting with no one. I had no one to call. I had no one calling me. I yearned for a full email inbox, as crazy as that sounds.

Compounding the stress was the fact that Whitney was early in her pregnancy at the time. I frequently wondered if I had made the biggest mistake of my professional life.

As my self-imposed ninety-day deadline rapidly approached, I had zero clients. I had zero *prospective* clients. In case you're wondering, zero clients equates to zero income. Not only was I making no money, I was spending money to get the business started.

I still didn't have a sense of what services I was offering. Imagine a sales conversation where you don't even know the services you're offering. Pathetic! Who was I kidding? I didn't even have sales conversations at the time because I had no one to talk to.

It was an absolute flop.

Interestingly, I noticed how I was talking to others about my business began to change. I didn't exude the same level of excitement that I had when I first started. I was more melancholy about it, defeated actually.

When someone would ask me about how it was going, I started saying, "Well, I'm not sure this was the right time to do this. My wife and I are expecting a child in a few months. I think it might be best to put this on hold for now, go back to work for someone else, and be better prepared for when the baby comes."

I would often try to convince myself that if I didn't put my business on hold, it was actually irresponsible of me, selfish even. I mean, I had nine months to prepare for a child and all the signs were pointing that I jumped the gun with this business venture.

It all made perfect sense to put the brakes on, didn't it? The timing wasn't right. My expertise wasn't right. The desire was there, but desire alone doesn't pay the bills. The result I got when I explained this to people was exactly what I wanted: a bunch of nodding heads who agreed with the decision. Notice the rationalization?

I contemplated tucking my tail between my legs, licking my wounds, and applying for a new job. Yet there was something within me that didn't feel right about giving up just yet.

I spent time reflecting on my situation. I tried to look objectively at what was working (which wasn't much) and where I could make improvements. In other words, I removed the emotion from the situation and explored it from a perspective of "problem-solution-opportunity."

After considerable self-analysis, I recognized that what was holding me back was actually something that had helped me in the past. I had a good track record of success in my professional life. I felt confident that if I were to find an open position that met my qualifications, I could submit my resume and get called for an interview. If I could get an interview, I had a good chance of getting offered a job. If I got offered a job, I wouldn't have to worry about being financially prepared for my child.

My resume was my ship. It was my safety net. It was my plan B. It was also holding me back. I decided to burn the ship. I deleted my resume.

It's easy for me to write these words now, but I assure you that carrying out such a ridiculous act was anything but easy. My hand lingered over the "move to trash" option on the screen. I was shaking in fear and disbelief, wondering if I should be medicated for even thinking such foolish thoughts.

I clicked the confirmation button and lowered my head. Immediately, I had buyer's remorse, except I didn't actually buy anything. I wondered what was wrong with me. I wondered why I would possibly do something so stupid, and decided to bury my face in my hands.

After a few seconds of self-pity, I sat up and looked at the computer screen. To my surprise and possibly delight, a box had popped up asking me, "Are you sure you want to delete this?"

Was this a sign from God? I wondered. Was He trying to tell me something? Was I being rescued?

"Are you sure you want to delete this?" What a ridiculous question to ask. No, I'm not sure I want to delete this. I'm not sure of anything.

I mentally battled with myself. I contemplated the decision over and over again. Finally, I clicked "Yes."

It was done. My resume was gone.

I'd like to report that in that exact moment, Google called and asked me to coach and train their entire company. That would be nice to write. It was also be an absolute lie. The phone didn't ring. I stared at a blank screen. I still had no clients and no one to call.

A strange sensation did come over me, however. While feeling completely terrified that I made an awful decision, I also felt an overwhelming sense of absolute freedom. No longer was I going to spend half of my time working on my business and the other half looking for employment opportunities. By closing one door, I committed myself wholeheartedly to the other.

That was more than five years ago, and I couldn't be happier with the decision.

Ships take many forms. In a professional setting, a ship could refer to a process that hasn't been updated in years. It becomes "the way it's always been done" and potentially prevents you from exploring whether there is a more efficient and effective way of doing something.

A ship could refer to the competent employee whose bad attitude brings the morale down for everyone else. Their negativity is tolerated because what they do for an organization is deemed more valuable than the negative atmosphere they create.

Another example could be the high paying client who provides a steady income for your business. The client is far from ideal. They actively prevent you from doing your best work. They don't appreciate your efforts. They never seem pleased with the product or service. They're unrealistic with their expectations. Seeing their number appear on your phone or seeing them scheduled on the calendar makes you want to call in sick.

It's time to embrace the crazy.

Burning the ships. Selling the mills. Deleting the resume. Changing old procedures. Firing a competent employee. Dismissing the high paying client. What do all of these instances have in common? In each example there are people, even yourself possibly, who look at those actions and think, "That's crazy."

Those who act in a bold manner are rarely offered permission or encouragement by those who are more content to marinate in conformity and complacency. That's exactly why I want you to embrace the crazy.

Embracing the crazy is an internal belief that you'll be okay and you'll land on your feet. Where you land may look different than what you thought, but you'll adapt. Too many people wait until they have all the answers before they launch. If there are ten items needed, they wait until all ten are in their possession. I would rather jump with eight and collect nine and ten while traveling.

It's about confidence. Confidence to try, to risk, to fail, to succeed. You may never recognize the extent of your greatness if you actively choose to never be tested with a challenge. Burning the ships will not guarantee success. Neither does conformity. I choose the former over the latter any day of the week.

DO THE WORK—OWN THE RESULTS

Regarding personal growth and development, many people will never advance beyond what I consider to be the foundational level of progress: Interest.

The internet has created a tremendous opportunity to obtain more information on just about every topic imaginable. Want to find out more about playing the guitar? Search the internet. Want to breed sea horses in your home? Search the internet. Want to learn how to get more dates? Search the internet.

This level of interest, while awesome in many respects, can also be a limitation. Acquiring more knowledge may or may not change your life. It can also provide a false sense of wisdom. Some people believe they know "everything" about a subject because they read a blog post about it somewhere. Never mind that most readers never check the validity or credibility of the author of the blog post. If it's on the internet, it must be true.

To truly grow and develop requires that we move to the next level of progress: Investment.

The advancement from the interest level to the investment level is evident in how you spend your time, your money, your energy, and your focus on a particular topic. The biggest shift within one who jumps to the next level occurs in their level of commitment to the topic.

Let's use webinars as an example. If you've ever hosted a webinar, you know that providing a free webinar will typically result in a higher number of participant registrations. However, at the time you conduct your webinar, those who actually attend will be far less than the number who registered. The formula is higher registrations and lower attendance.

If you charge a fee to attend a webinar, even a nominal fee, you're likely to get fewer people to register. You'll have a higher percentage of people who attend at the time of the webinar, however. The formula is lower registrations and higher attendance.

Of course, there's nothing wrong with either group of people. It's completely acceptable for someone to investigate a topic before committing to it. But over time, the first group tends to attract inquirers, dabblers, and people who are simply "checking it out." They're the window shopping customers. They're the "just looking" crowd.

The second group consists more of the doers. They ante up, and they're now investigating and learning from a more committed lens.

Who gets more excited when a professor cancels a class, the kids who attend college on their parents' dime or the ones who are paying for their education out of their own pocket? Again, not right or wrong. Just different levels of commitment.

The road to significance requires an investment. It requires that you focus your efforts on achieving something meaningful. We cannot stay at the dabbler level and think we're going make a dent. Give yourself wholly to your commitment, so that you do not succumb to the temptation to merely pursue the path of least resistance. Instead, pursue the path of most significance.

Just as a focused effort is required to create a life of significance, so too, does it require certain sacrifices. This mantra that "you can have it all" seems delightful, doesn't it? Who doesn't want it all? I think most people would opt for that, but not everyone is willing to do what's necessary to have it all. Are you willing to make sacrifices to achieve that which is most meaningful in your life?

If you prefer to stay where you are, all right. At minimum, stay where you are, but approach what you're doing and how you're doing it with a reinvigorated spirit. You don't have to make major career changes to kick start your life, unless that's what you've been contemplating in your mind. You can easily evaluate where you are, be confident in your choice to stay where you are, and declare to make the people and world around you better.

Own that choice if that is your desire. It's far better to travel that route than to either begrudgingly stay in your own discomfort or to pursue a new venture with a tempered spirit. Lukewarm efforts are more repulsive than a proactive choice to remain stagnant. Half-assed commitments generate half-assed results.

Before embracing the crazy, it's important to assess your current skill set. Yet it's equally as important to assess whether you possess the resolve, discipline and determination to learn the necessary skill set that may be required of you in the future.

For the wanna-be entrepreneur, what matters to me more is not whether you presently *know* how to market your product or service. I'm more interested in whether you're willing to throw yourself into *learning* everything you can about how to succeed.

For those contemplating a career jump, I'm not as interested in whether you know everything there is to know about the role of the new position. I'm more interested in whether you can commit to learning the new role like an expert.

ONE QUESTION

Let's simplify this. Before my stroke, I wanted to be *successful*. I had a six-figure salary, I managed a huge team, and I was (and still am) blessed with a woman and family who loved me. I could have done more, but I was comfortable. Things were good.

Since my stroke, my focus has changed: I want to have a life of *significance*, and I mean that in a big way. Because you're reading this, you do, too.

Much of our behavior, and therefore our results, is determined by how we answer one question:

Will you choose "Why bother?" Or will you choose "Why not?"

It seems like such a simple question, doesn't it? It's almost as if a question so simple couldn't possibly make such a significant difference in our lives. But it does.

In instances when we choose, "Why bother?" it's evident, both mentally and physically, we allow our fears, self-doubts, or insecurities to minimize our truest ambitions and deepest desires.

When choosing this option, we're inclined to blame others, make excuses, procrastinate, rationalize our current situation, ignore things that need our attention, label ourselves perfectionists, complain about things we don't control, or engage in other self-defensive measures, all with the intent to protect ourselves.

The contrasting choice is, "Why not?"

This option requires that we ask ourselves, "What would be possible if...?" for every situation. Risk and uncertainty are undoubtedly present, yet so are feelings of being challenged and excited.

The "Why not?" option offers no promises and no guarantees of success. Quite the contrary, the risk of failure is abundantly present with almost every meaningful endeavor.

Yet, as challenging an option as this can be, as much as it removes us from what is familiar and comfortable, deep down it is the option that tugs at our hearts, almost begging us to choose it.

Let's be clear: The "Why not?" option isn't a safer choice. It's just the one that leads to significance, the one that allows us to boldly proclaim that who we are and what we do matters.

No one ever achieved significance by playing it safe. Life wasn't meant to be played safe. The choice is yours. Will you choose "Why bother?" or will you choose "Why not?"?

8

NOT ABOUT YOU

"I don't know what your destiny will be, but one thing I know: the only ones among you who will be really happy are those who will have sought and found how to serve."

~ Albert Schweitzer

People sometimes say things in an attempt to sound inspiring but are actually quite silly.

I often hear speakers say, "If I can change the life of just one person in the audience during my presentation, I've done my job well." If you're a speaker with a meaningful message to share and you only change the life of one person during your presentation, you probably shouldn't be invited back. Sorry to sound harsh, but what the heck happened to the other ninety-nine percent of the audience?

People say that if they are able to change the life of just one other person during their lifetime, it is a life well lived. Great idea, except that when you're born, you've already affected the lives of at least two people. Let's keep the momentum going. If you only change one life, you're somehow retreating.

Most of what is covered in this book is about *you*. It's about taking a look in the mirror and figuring out how to better the person looking back. It's about understanding that we all have our own gifts, our own struggles, and our own desires. It's about believing that the extent of your impact may be directly proportionate to your level of self-awareness and desire to improve.

In order to manifest the amazing things you were created for, it starts with you. But at no point was it ever about you.

Self-awareness is constructive.

Self-absorption is destructive.

I have taught, encouraged, and challenged you to become more boldly self-expressed, to remove the internal barriers that prevent you from being a light in the world that seems to, on occasion, become perpetually darker.

We're created to be connected to others, to live in community. We're created to be ourselves, innately gifted with our unique attributes that can positively impact the lives of others. There's no magic number in terms of how many lives we need to change in order to qualify for the proverbial "Lifetime of Significance" award. But to be content to settle for one life changed is minimizing what you're capable of doing. You were created for more than that. Much more.

This isn't about trying to please everyone. It's definitely not about living a watered-down version of yourself for the sake of acceptance and conformity. It's about recognizing the more boldly self-expressed you are, the better connected you become to those with whom you are meant to serve.

People want to know that who they are and what they do matters. One way they get that confirmation is through their contributions and believing that they're making a difference in this world.

It connects back to what you choose your life to be about.

This is your stand.

Your stand, your purpose, cannot be for your own benefit. If you are truly living out your stand, you'll recognize that others around you benefit as well. Knowing that you are living a life of contribution generates more internal engagement and motivation than any professional incentive program ever could superficially and temporarily produce.

Sadly, many people don't recognize or believe that they are contributing much to the world around them. Some mistakenly believe that it's their type of job that determines the level of their impact. Only people who sell their homes in order to go and work for an orphanage in Africa are truly significant, they think.

They fail to understand that we can live significantly in both what we do and how we do it. No organizational chart dictates the level of your contribution in the things that matter most. Entry level employees can be just as inspirational to others as the top executives. And your age doesn't represent the scale of your influence.

What makes our stand so powerful is the belief that, upon living it, it actually makes a difference in the lives of others. To live purposefully is to contribute greatly. If you remove the sense of purpose or the belief of contribution from someone, you will witness the light go out in their eyes and see a defeated demeanor in their actions. Ultimately, what may be diagnosed as depression might also be despair and disconnection.

WHAT ARE YOU GIVING?

As you would imagine, living a life of significance requires a certain sense of giving to others. But by "giving" I do not solely mean giving your time or your money, though both of those gifts can create a tremendous impact for others. There's more to it than that.

Have you ever met someone who gives and gives and gives? If the act of giving directly resulted in joyous emotions, then a person like this should have a smile on their face that circumnavigates the globe. Yet at times these people are exhausted and flustered, and they seem to gain no personal enjoyment from their giving. What gives?

Not all giving is equal.

Needless to say, your attitude, your mentality, and your state of giving will determine your level of satisfaction and fulfillment.

If you've ever eaten at a Chick-fil-A restaurant, you'll know that their servers are trained to say "my pleasure" when being thanked by a patron. This is to help create a culture of people who find joy in giving to others. Not out of obligation. Not out of expectation. Simply the joy of giving.

Giving from a sense of obligation won't generate a sense of connection and contribution. Being forced to give can even create resentment.

Giving now to receive later is nothing more than "tit-for-tat," creating an expectation for a favor to be returned at a point in the future. When the act isn't reciprocated, any joy we have initially experienced is quickly eradicated.

Giving out of guilt is not empowering. Donating because you feel like you "should" won't cause your "cup of joy" to bubble over anytime soon.

In his book *The Charge*, author Brendon Burchard[7] does a great job differentiating between giving of and giving to. He writes, "I've come to realize that contributing to the world doesn't always have to be a social affair. I bring this to light because too many people think of contributing as simply giving to something specific, so they never feel that they contribute to the world except when a Girl Scout shows up at the door hawking cookies. Ours is a society that has falsely assumed that contribution must mean giving to some specific cause rather than simply giving of our best selves. Thus, too many people don't recognize the fact that simply being who they are is contributing significantly to the world."

Imagine the influence and difference you could make in your immediate situation if you just lived out your core words and your core stand more frequently! You would be an inspiration to others not only by *what you do* but by *who you are*.

Businesses thrive when they first focus on who shows up. The attitudes, the energy, and the enthusiasm of the employees are often clear indicators of the level of success of the organization.

Your presence alone generates feelings within others. When you enter a room, are people excited that you're there? Do they get a sense of comfort? Do they think all is well? Or do they think the wheels are about to fall off because you decided to attend the meeting?

Athletes inspire fans by giving of themselves. I'm inspired by Cal Ripken because he's the record holder for most consecutive baseball games played. To consider what he accomplished is amazing. His record makes today's athletes seem fragile and pampered, in comparison.

Singers can move people by giving of themselves. To listen to Whitney Houston perform "The Star-Spangled Banner" at the Super Bowl XXV still gives me goosebumps. In my opinion, her rendition is one of the greatest of all time.

Have you heard Carrie Underwood and Vince Gill sing "How Great Thou Art" together? Can you not help but feel the emotions rise within you when listening to it? Their rendition is so good, they got a standing ovation during the performance. They weren't even finished with the song yet.

Neither Cal, nor Whitney, nor Carrie ever gave anything to me directly. But by being who they are and sharing their gifts with the world, their impact can be measured in the millions.

I don't mean to minimize or ignore the impact one can have by giving to something or someone, either. When we use our resources, including our time and money, to benefit the life of someone else, we can be as fulfilled as the recipient of our offering.

Your money, used intentionally to benefit others, can leave a lasting impression. You don't have to break the bank to make a difference.

I was once asked to be the closing keynote speaker at a conference in Clearwater, Florida. Because my session was scheduled for late Thursday morning, my wife and I decided to turn the event into an extended weekend family vacation. I had Whitney and the boys fly down Thursday afternoon to meet me.

On our last night, we decided to eat at a nice restaurant for dinner. Sitting at the next table was an older couple who were out celebrating their anniversary. We engaged in small chatter about the kids, and I apologized in advance for what would most assuredly no longer be a quiet dinner outing for them.

We ordered our food and drinks and started playing the game parents play with their hungry kids at nice restaurants: The "How long can I keep you entertained before your food comes so you don't tantrum and embarrass the hell out of me?" game. And you thought Sudoko was challenging!

While waiting for our food, the couple next to us commented about how well behaved the boys were, and how it was nice to hear the laughter of children again. I appreciated the compliment, but I wasn't satisfied with my kids' behavior. I thought they were acting up a bit more than I preferred.

If you think time flies when you're having fun, you should check out what time does when your kids are tired, hungry, and can't do anything but wait to be served. Time stands still. Seconds become minutes and minutes seem like hours.

The kids' food finally arrived. Whitney and I helped the boys finish most of their meals and waited patiently for our meals to get served. Five minutes became ten minutes. Ten minutes became twenty minutes. The boys were getting restless. They broke out in a wrestling match in our booth. I started snarling like an angry wolf. My eyes grew wide, my teeth became clenched, and I felt like a rabid animal ready to pounce.

Finally, our food was served. At the same time, I heard the couple behind me saying goodbye to the waitress. On their way out, they stopped by our table to wish us a safe return back home.

Normally I'd be excited for such a conversation but I wasn't as chatty this time. I was polite, but I didn't reciprocate the conversation. I was upset that the food took so long to be served. I was upset that my boys couldn't keep it together in public. We said goodbye and quickly finished our meal.

Our waitress came back to check on us. "How is everything over here?" she asked.

"It's great. I think we're all set. I'll take the check, please."

"Wonderful. I just wanted to let you know that your meal has been paid for," she said.

"What?" I asked. "What do you mean?"

"The couple that just left bought your dinner tonight. I wanted to let you know but I wasn't allowed to say anything until they left," she said.

We quickly turned to see if the couple was still there, but they were gone. I didn't quite know what to say. They just bought dinner for my family, yet it was their anniversary. It was humbling, and I felt somewhat embarrassed that I didn't spend more time chatting with them. I wondered if they'd ever realize the impact of their generosity.

The actions of that couple represent what it means to live a significant life. It's the simple gestures we exhibit when we are at our best that make the biggest impact in the lives of others.

Of course, not all significant endeavors require a monetary payment. One of the most rewarding experiences of my life came during my time spent as a high school wrestling coach.

Wrestling is a tough sport. The joy, the satisfaction, and the fulfillment in winning a match are exhilarating. It's something I wish every person could experience at least once in their life. I used to believe that there was no better feeling than when the referee raised your arm in victory.

I was wrong.

There is something magical about coaching. It is a humbling and honoring experience. In many respects, teaching other wrestlers and helping them achieve their own success proved to be much more challenging than when I was competing myself. It also proved to be much more rewarding.

The young men I had the privilege to coach will forever have a place in my heart. Their impact on me wasn't proportionate to the level of success they had in wrestling. It's just as easy for me to rattle off the names of my state champions, state finalists, and state place winners as it is for me to tell stories about those who had no business ever stepping onto a wrestling mat.

It's the relationships, the connections, the discipline, and the sacrifices made by every one of us that create bonds that last a lifetime. It is the willingness to invest yourself in the life of someone else without the expectation of anything in return that often makes us feel like we're doing our most significant work.

It's in situations like that when you realize that your personal success, while great, is not the greatest level of fulfillment. That moment, at least in the wrestling arena, is when you witness someone you've trained, coached, and loved getting their hand raised in victory. That is the ultimate high.

In retrospect, what I gave to the athletes was my time, my knowledge, and a desire to help them be successful in their own careers. What they gave back to me far outweighed my investment in them. They gave me meaning, purpose, and fulfillment.

Giving of yourself and giving to others starts with you. It's not about you.

One person who exemplifies what it means to give in an extraordinary manner is my friend Michael Port. Michael is a six-time *New York Times* best-selling author, top rated speaker, and trusted mentor.

I've had the privilege of working with Michael for a number of years, beginning when I enrolled in his *Book Yourself Solid* program. At the time, I was struggling in my business. Michael's program and guidance helped me get my business to where it is today.

I don't normally travel through the land of the rich and famous and I don't know any media celebrities. In the world of speakers, consultants, and coaches, however, Michael is a legend.

He would be embarrassed if he knew I called him that, which is what makes him so likable. Michael has a great sense of humility about him. In every engagement, he is consistently genuine in word and action. I find that refreshing.

Achieving a tremendous level of success as a speaker and author of *Book Yourself Solid*, Michael recently branched out into the world of teaching people how to become better speakers themselves. His latest book, *Steal the Show*, reached *The Wall Street Journal, USA Today and Publisher's Weekly* best-seller lists. It seems like a no-brainer, then, that his *Heroic Public Speaking* program would be successful, and it is. But there's more to the story—and him—than that.

In the early years of my business, Michael was headlining Entrepreneur Magazine's Thought-Leaders Live conference in Arlington, Virginia. It was a local event for me, and I was excited to attend.

After the conference, I had the opportunity to join Michael and another speaker for lunch. While we ate, I listened as Michael and the other speaker talked about their respective businesses. Though I was clearly not as well established as either of them, they were kind enough to ask me about what I envisioned for my own business, and they listened attentively.

As we discussed different ideas, what struck me most about the conversation was the tone. At no point did a negative word or a negative thought ever get mentioned. Ever.

Living in the Washington, D.C. area, there's certainly plenty of opportunity to find something negative to discuss. Yet in this conversation, everything we discussed was framed within the "what's possible" mindset. It wasn't planned that way. It naturally evolved. It was one of the most positive, uplifting conversations I've ever had.

During that lunch, Michael talked about what was next for him. The *Book Yourself Solid* system was essentially running itself by that point. He was ready for the next adventure, though admittedly he wasn't sure exactly what that looked like.

Less than a year later, while attending one of his regional *Book Yourself Solid* coaching programs, Michael first introduced the idea of creating a program designed to help people deliver better performances in their lives. I enrolled in his pilot program, and the *Heroic Public Speaking* program has been off to the races ever since.

When Michael rolled out the HPS program, he talked about the fear associated with it. At first, I was somewhat shocked to hear that. How could someone who was already such a success be worried about this new endeavor?

However, it was because of his success in one area that created the fear about entering another arena. In his mind, the possibility of producing a flop with HPS could possibly damage his reputation and success with BYS. It was a perspective I hadn't considered because I wasn't exactly at Michael's level of success. It showed that regardless of the level of success you've achieved, the voice of the internal critic will always be there to greet you. The fact that he was sharing that with us was yet another example of his authenticity.

As he says in his "The Think Big Revolution" keynote presentation, "I stand for thinking bigger about who you are and about what you offer the world. See, I want to think bigger in my world and I want to help you think bigger in yours. Everything I do in my work and my personal life is driven by this purpose."

It shows.

Today, Michael gives of himself in every endeavor and gives to those with whom he is meant to serve. Both HPS and BYS are widely successful because of it.

Finally, my last example of someone who gives of himself to others is Joe Moravsky. If you live in the Connecticut area, you might recognize Joe as a meteorologist on television. If not, you may also recognize him from the *American Ninja Warrior* competitions.

I first heard of Joe as *American Ninja Warrior* played in the background on the TV one night at my house. I was writing this book, not paying much attention to the program, until they started interviewing Joe. I put the pen down and was enthralled with his story.

"This used to be just about me and how well I could do, but through the years I've met some people that have changed my life," Joe said in his interview.[8] Specifically, one of those people who drastically shifted his perspective was a young fan, a little girl with stage four neuroblastoma cancer. Sadly, just a few months after meeting his biggest fan, she passed away.

"I do this for people like that, to be able to change their life. The funny thing is, they change my life," he said.

I had the chance to speak with Joe about his experiences. He offered a wonderful perspective on why he competes for those struggling with life-threatening illnesses. He said, "Some people need money so you give them money. Some people need a friend, and I can be a friend. But those faced with a terminal illness are different. There's just something about being a part of their lives for the time they have left. To be able to elevate them from happy to ecstatic in their final days is so much more meaningful to me. That's the great thing about *American Ninja Warrior*. It's given me a platform to change people's lives in a meaningful way."

What is remarkable about Joe is that he possesses what each and every one of has within us. We may not have the physical attribute or stamina that he has. We do have the opportunity to broaden our perspective, to recognize that we receive fulfillment ourselves when we bring fulfillment to others. Through being who we are and pursuing what we find to be most meaningful, we will change the world, one person at a time.

I have shared examples of individuals who are living a life of significance. I would be remiss, however, if I didn't also include an example of an entire community of people who epitomize what it means to give of yourself to others. For that, we need not look any further than those who proudly serve in our military.

I have never served in the military, though I have family and friends who do. To know that there are people who willingly dedicate themselves to a cause bigger than themselves is admirable. Not only that, to do so in a way that requires tremendous individual sacrifice, discipline, and honor is what makes who they are and what they do so remarkable.

Significance.

Regardless of where you are in your life, you have learned and experienced things that others haven't.

Students in middle school may wonder how you successfully kept your reputation intact, even with the ills of social media.

Maybe a girl is contemplating getting a tattoo of her boyfriend's name on her face. Your insight on why that might not be a great idea could save her quite a bit of embarrassment in the future.

Start-up entrepreneurs may wonder what you've learned through your own business experience.

Parents of newborns can learn from parents with older kids.

The list is endless.

Look for ways to mentor, to coach, to teach, to train, willingly. You have something to contribute, and others want to learn. Bless and be blessed.

If you are a leader of a team or company, you're already in a position of authority, and therefore possess a great opportunity to influence those around you. The mistake made by many ineffective leaders and managers, however, is that they exert their authority *because* of their position. There's nothing significant about a manager on a power trip. It's actually quite repulsive.

The best leaders and managers are those who possess the ability to tap into what's most meaningful for the employees, based on what the employees have declared for themselves. It requires first that the manager cares. I recognize how obvious that sounds, yet it's remarkable how many managers believe that they're there to get a job done, not to be friends with the employees. This is astounding to me. I'm not suggesting that every employee becomes a beer drinking buddy, but what harm is there in treating your employees as well as you'd treat your friends? Great leadership starts with you, but it's never about you.

Perhaps you're an employee who's not in a leadership or management position. Must you wait until you achieve a position or title to be a person of influence? Absolutely not. Again, by taking a stand and living out your stand, you will attract people's attention. Standing for something builds you up and provides an example to others that they can do the same for themselves. Excellence starts with you, but it's never about you.

At times, standing for something might be contrary to what the masses are doing. It's easy for employees to complain about management. It's easy to stay stuck by joining in the negative rhetoric. Yet it's precisely in those moments when people who take a stand are able to lift others from the depths of despair and into a more proactive, healthier environment. Creating a movement, a shift, a revolution starts with you. It's just not about you.

Significance.

As you examine your life, where are you giving of yourself? Are you living each moment representing your core words and living out your core stand?

Where are you giving to others? If you have been blessed with financial resources, consider ways to use that to bless the life of another.

Can you allocate your time to be spent in endeavors that provide value to someone else? Look for ways to coach, to mentor, to train someone else, without any expectations for what they can do for you.

Giving of yourself and giving to others starts with you. It's not about you.

Living a life of significance starts with you, but it is never about you.

9

SEE YOUR SIGNIFICANCE

"Tell me, what do you see?"

~ Johann Lombard

I met Johann at an airport in Michigan during a layover. I had a few minutes before my connecting flight and I decided to grab a quick lunch.

I ordered my meal and sat at an open table. Seeing an available seat, Johann asked if he could join me. I'm so glad he did.

After a few minutes of chatting about the food and airport, I found out that Johann had one of the coolest jobs I could ever imagine: safari tour guide!

Instantly, I became a five-year-old kid. I was enamored with his job and asked him to tell me all about lions, elephants, and every other wild animal that came to mind. It was like having the Animal Planet network wrapped into one person, without the commercials.

I learned that Johann started off as a tour guide and now teaches other guides how to give tours. When I asked him about how and why he made that transition, his answer took me by surprise. "I gave a tour to a blind man," he said.

"What?" I asked.

He started laughing at the sight of my reaction.

"That's the same look and question I had when he came to my camp," he said. "I didn't know what to do. The biggest attraction for most tour participants is getting a chance to visually see the animals. I didn't know what to do with this person."

I was hooked. I couldn't fathom what I would do in that situation, and I was dying to find out how Johann handled it. This is his story he told me:

I asked the gentleman what he wanted to do. He told me he wanted to see the lions. Begrudgingly, I took him in my Jeep to where the lions were resting. I parked about fifty meters away from them and turned off the engine.

"We're here," I told him.

"Tell me, what do you see?" he asked me.

I said, "I see lions about fifty meters away. There's one male surrounded by four females. All are lying in the grass."

I thought that was sufficient. It wasn't.

"No, no. Tell me. What do you *see*?" the man insisted.

I wondered if it mattered what I could see. This

man couldn't see anything anyway. However, I decided to give some more description.

"The lions see us, though they don't seem very interested. There's a small body of water near them. There are birds flying overhead. Out in the distance, there are elephants, not too close to the lions."

I figured surely that was plenty of information for him. Not so.

"No, no," the man said softly. He stood up in the Jeep. "Tell me, what do you see?" he asked, as he waved his arm from left to right.

Admittedly, I was a little annoyed, yet also intrigued. I stepped back and suddenly saw the entire scene differently. I started describing the view from a panoramic perspective. I described what was to the north, south, east, and west of us.

I talked about the mountain range off in the distance, and how the grassy fields seemed to go on for miles. I described the location of the sun, and the reflections it created on the land.

I described the wooded area, and the animals that were most likely lounging in there, remaining out of sight of the lions.

I described everything I could to a man who could see none of it.

He seemed content with that description. "I want to smell them," he said.

I started the Jeep and drove downwind, stopping roughly twenty-five meters from the lions.

We sat in silence for a short time. Suddenly, the man stood in the Jeep, raised his head to the sky, inhaled deeply, and burst into tears. "I see them now," he said.

Since that tour, I've never looked at what I do in the same way. I am driven to teach other guides what I learned in that moment, so that they can describe more than what the untrained eye sees during their tours.

Johann's story inspired me, and I often tell it during my speaking presentations. I think it speaks to those moments when we get so focused on what's immediately before us and we fail to step back to see the bigger picture.

It's easy to stay stuck in life's difficult situations without recognizing that it is precisely because of those moments when we get to exhibit our courage, our resilience, and our resolve.

It's easy to focus on the argument yet lose track of the relationship.

It's easy to focus on the income yet lose sight of the impact.

It's easy to feel like we don't matter, yet that is precisely what we are called to do.

It's easy to think this life is about us and forget that we are but a piece of a larger creation.

It's easy to settle for success instead of relentlessly pursuing significance.

It's easy to stay blind when every fiber in our bodies yearns to see.

Now, dear reader, it's your turn. Tell me, what do you see?

ACKNOWLEDGMENTS

It doesn't seem possible to adequately thank all those who contributed, directly and indirectly, to the creation of this book. What is very possible, however, is recognizing the tremendous influence you have all had on my life.

To Whitney — Your love and support continue to expand beyond the horizon. Today and always, I look at you with humble adoration. You are simply amazing.

To Finnegan and Declan — You are my daily reminder that there is little in this world more gratifying than seeing the joy in a child's eyes. You are my boys, and my heart has never contained so much love as it does for you.

To Dad, Mom and the rest of my family — If I had to list you all, it would read like the genealogy section of Genesis in the Bible. It would also double the number of pages in this book. Please know that I love you all.

To my friends — Though our experiences together have ranged from celebrating the birth of a child to consoling another through the death of a loved one, who you are as an individual is what continues to be a tremendous influence in my life today.

To those that have allowed me to serve you professionally — Witnessing the transformation in your lives as you become focused on living a life of significance brings me more joy, satisfaction, and fulfillment than you could ever imagine. I only hope that I might do the same for you. Thank you for allowing me to serve you.

Lastly, I would be remiss if I didn't acknowledge the one true God. It is because of you that I am still here. You continue to bless me, even in those moments I doubt my worth. You raise me up, encourage me, and challenge me to be more than I can be. You are truly the great I AM.

NOTES

[1]HyperionBooksVideos's channel, "Liz Murray talks about going from Homeless to Harvard." Online video clip. YouTube.com. Posted August 30, 2010. *https://www.youtube.com/watch?v=EtybvFWoncY*

[2]Greitens, Eric *Resilience.* City: Houghton Mifflin Harcourt; 2015; page 81

[3]Williamson, Marianne *A Return to Love: Reflections on the Principles of "A Course in Miracles;" HarperOne; 1996*

[4]Nepo, Mark, *The Book of Awakening: Having the Life You Want by Being Present to the Life You Have; Conari Press; 2000*

[5]The Mayo Clinic website citation.... http://www.mayoclinic.org/healthy-lifestyle/adult-health/in-depth/forgiveness/art-20047692

[6]Collins, Jim *Good to Great;* HarperCollins; 2001; Page 17

[7]Burchard, Brendon *The Charge;* Free Press; 2012; page 205

[8]America Ninja Warrior ... https://www.facebook.com/JoeMoravsky/videos/ 1232958473402594/